KEEP ON BELIEVING

Dr. Robert H. Schuller

KEEP ON BELIEVING

Hour of Power Publishers
Garden Grove, California 92642

7 85

This book is dedicated to . . .

the nearly 1000 workers and volunteers who help me in my Hour of Power ministry. To each of these people this book is dedicated.

FOREWORD

Christmas is a difficult time for many people. Every year I receive desperate letters and urgent telephone calls from folks who are filled with sorrow, wracked with pain and frightened with loneliness.

They are full of unhappy memories . . .

. . . spending Christmas alone for the first time after the death of a loved one . . .

. . . children grown up and not coming home

. . . the pain of a recent divorce . . .

And they find that the holidays are almost impossible to bear.

They need to keep on believing, and find the joy of the Christ child bringing love and new hope.

And they can!

That's why I've written this book inspired by the sayings of Jesus.

I invite you as you read this book to re-examine your relationship with the Greatest Possibility Thinker that ever lived—Jesus Christ. He can make your best times better: and your worst times wonderful experiences with God!

Robert Schuller

Garden Grove, California
Christmas, 1976

11

CONTENTS

Here is real Happiness . . .

3   "Blessed are the poor in spirit, for theirs is the kingdom of heaven.

4   "Blessed are those who mourn, for they shall be comforted.

5   "Blessed are the meek, for they shall inherit the earth.

6   "Blessed are those who hunger and thirst for righteousness, for they shall be satisfied.

7   "Blessed are the merciful, for they shall obtain mercy.

8   "Blessed are the pure in heart, for they shall see God.

9   "Blessed are the peacemakers, for they shall be called sons of God.

10   "Blessed are those who are persecuted for righteousness' sake, for their is the kingdom of heaven."

(Matthew 5:3-10)
Revised Standard Version

3   "Blessed are the poor in spirit: for theirs is the kingdom of heaven.

4   Blessed are they that mourn: for they shall be comforted.

5   Blessed are the meek: for they shall inherit the earth.

6   Blessed are they which do hunger and thirst after righteousness: for they shall be filled.

7   Blessed are the merciful: for they shall obtain mercy.

8   Blessed are the pure in heart: for they shall see God.

9   Blessed are the peacemakers: for they shall be called the children of God.

10   Blessed are they which are persecuted for righteousness' sake: for theirs is the kingdom of heaven.''

(Matthew 5:3-10)
King James Version

"How happy are the humble-minded, for the kingdom of Heaven is theirs!

"How happy are those who know what sorrow means, for they will be given courage and comfort!

"Happy are those who claim nothing, for the whole earth will belong to them!

"Happy are those who are hungry and thirsty for goodness, for they will be fully satisfied!

"Happy are the merciful, for they will have mercy shown to them!

"Happy are the utterly sincere, for they will see God!

"Happy are those who make peace, for they will be known as sons of God!

"Happy are those who have suffered persecution for the cause of goodness, for the kingdom of Heaven is theirs!

(Matthew 5:3-10)
Phillips Translation

3 "Humble men are very fortunate!" he told them, "for the Kingdom of Heaven is given to them.

4 Those who mourn are fortunate! for they shall be comforted.

5 The meek and lowly are fortunate! for the whole wide world belongs to them.

6 "Happy are those who long to be just and good, for they shall be completely satisfied.

7 Happy are the kind and merciful, for they shall be shown mercy.

8 Happy are those whose hearts are pure, for they shall see God.

9 Happy are those who strive for peace—they shall be called the sons of God.

10 Happy are those who are persecuted because they are good, for the Kingdom of Heaven is theirs.

(Matthew 5:3-10)
The Living Translation

3　Happy are those with an inferior consciousness, because the Kingdom of heaven comes from them.

4　Happy are those that mourn, because they will receive encouragement.

5　Happy are the gentle, because they will be given the earth.

6　Happy are those who hunger and thirst for righteousness because they will be fed.

7　Happy are the merciful, because they will receive compassion.

8　Happy are those with a clean heart, because they will see God.

9　Happy are those making peace, because they will be called Sons of God.

10　Happy are those who are persecuted for the sake of righteousness, because the Kingdom of Heaven comes from them.

(Matthew 5:3-10)
Translated from the
original Greek by
Dr. Schuller's son,
Robert A. Schuller.

CHAPTER ONE

Happiness is not a matter of not having problems . . .

. . . it is a matter of having problems and knowing how to handle them!

"Blessed are the poor in spirit, for theirs is the kingdom of heaven."

(Matt. 5:3)

I

Take the First Step to Happiness

I watched an interview recently on television of a woman on the streets of New York City. She was obviously overweight, over-rushed, over-tense. The interviewer asked her if she was happy. She snapped, "Who's happy today? Everybody has so many problems." With that she rushed on down the street. I wanted to speak up, "Wait a minute, whoever you are. Happiness is not a question of having or not having problems. Everyone has problems."

I was in the home and the office of a man whose personal fortune is measured in the tens of millions of dollars. Yet he has financial problems. Everybody faces financial problems, it seems. I read about a man who lost his credit card. He said, "I don't think I will report it, though, because the person who found it is spending less than my wife did!"

HAPPINESS IS NOT A MATTER OF NOT HAVING PROBLEMS . . .

. . . IT IS A MATTER OF HAVING PROBLEMS AND KNOWING HOW TO HANDLE THEM!

It's a matter of going to the right people and dealing with them, if you will, in the right way. You've heard about the man whose doctor said, "You worry too much; that is your trouble. Whistle while you work." The man replied, "I can't; I am a skin diver!"

Another man went to his doctor and the doctor was very helpful. The doctor said, "I am sure I have the answer to your problem." The man answered, "I certainly hope so, doctor. I should have come to you long ago." The doctor asked,

"Where did you go?" The man said, "I went to the druggist." The doctor said, "What kind of foolish advice did he give you?" The man replied, "He said, 'Go see your doctor.'"

We do go to the wrong places too often. If you have a medical problem, go to your doctor. I have a spiritual doctor that I recommend. His name is Jesus Christ. Believe me, Jesus Christ was a joy-filled person and He had problems; but He knew how to handle them creatively and constructively.

If you will follow me through the next eight chapters as we look upon the Beatitudes of Jesus Christ, you will discover our Lord's key to joyful living. You will get high on happiness, and that is healthy living.

Jesus said, "Blessed are the poor in spirit, for theirs is the kingdom of heaven." (Matt. 5:3) As we study this Beatitude I want you to think first about the *promise* that is in this text, then the *problems that stand in the way*, then the *principle* that is inherent in His command, and finally the *path* that you can take to take advantage of the principles that He teaches.

First, there is the promise of Jesus Christ Himself that you can enjoy the kingdom of heaven. This does not mean simply that you will enjoy heaven in eternity after you pass away, after this earthly pilgrimage. It does mean heaven here and heaven now.

Batten, Barton, Durstine and Osborn, a New York City advertising agency, conducted a lengthy and very responsible poll on the relation between happiness and individuals. The study revealed that the happiest group of people are married women between the ages of 18 and 34. It further showed that religious people are five times happier than non-religious people.

I believe religion changes you and makes you a happier person. I wear a little sticker which symbolizes the secret of my happiness. It simply states, "I am third." I also have a little key with the word J-O-Y. "J" for Jesus, "O" for Others, and "Y" for Yourself. Put Jesus first, others second, yourself last and you will live a happy life.

The sticker says the same thing, "I am third." God is first, others come second and I am third. I pray that when people see this sticker they will begin to feel: "I am Third . . . I am Third . . . I am Third." This is a beginning toward overcoming the tension, trouble, animosity, jealousy, and difficulty which pervades the world today. Stop living by the creed: "I am first, others second, and God can come third." That is the sure road to hell on earth.

Happy is the man who realizes that in life he is poor unless . . .

GOD IS FIRST,

   OTHERS COME SECOND,

     AND HE IS THIRD!

Let us suppose you live by the principle, "I am

first." You decide to be first at a traffic intersection. You take chances passing and cutting in and out of lanes. You end up first in line, but in the process you may cause an accident and thereby ruin your own joy for the day. What did you gain?

Again, let us suppose you want to be at the head of a long line of waiting people. You push and elbow your way through on the "I am first" principle. You get to the front of the line, but are you really happy? Be willing to be third. That is what this Beatitude says, "Blessed are the poor in spirit, for theirs is the kingdom of heaven." (Matt. 5:3) No matter who you are or what your problem is, I promise you that if you live by the "I am third" principle and put God first, enormous joy can come into your life.

Let me share a letter with you that I received:

"Dear Dr. Schuller: This letter is a must, and I hope you will be able to read it personally. You, the New Hope telephone counselors, and Doctor Robert Merkle proved to me that God not only can work miracles, but He can really speed things up when necessary. Thirty days ago I reached bottom both spiritually and financially. I was out of work, sick, discouraged. I could see nothing but misery ahead. I was convinced that life was not worth living another day.

A close friend told me to watch the Hour of Power. I did. The sermon was inspirational and the service was beautiful. I was uplifted for the day, but the rest of the week was a nightmare.

Finally I became wretched enough to relent and honestly give God a chance.

"I first called the New Hope telephone line. A gracious gentle lady answered and tried to help me. She suggested that I come in to see one of the counselors as soon as possible. She said meanwhile she wanted to put my name on the church's prayer list because praying makes the difference. I am convinced that many people must have prayed for me because the following day miracles began to happen.

"First, a friend came by and offered to drive me to your church. I was concerned because I had no money to pay for counseling; but we drove over to the church anyway. As we walked toward the tower, I became nervous and wondered what to say.

At this moment the second miracle happened. A woman came out of the tower and started walking toward her car. She saw us and asked whether there was anything she could do to help. I blurted out, 'Do you help people who do not have money?' The immediate answer was, 'Of course. You are more important than money. Go into the lobby of the tower and tell the woman at the desk what your problem is. She will be glad to help you.' My friend and I went in and I explained my problem.

That is when the third miracle occurred. The woman at the desk called one of the counselors and found that there had been an unexpected cancellation and I could go right up for a consultation! As a result of my appointment with Dr. Merkle, God became real to me. I now know that God is the key to spiritual peace of mind. He is real; He is beautiful. I now have a part-time job; my financial burdens are lessened; my health is improved. In other words, my life is transformed!''

Now, you must understand the basic underlying principle. The promise is joy; the principle is the knowledge that without God, there is no joy. Without Him, you are promised nothing; you are finished. Blessed are the poor in spirit.

Happy is the man who, after sinking to the depths and finally losing all his false pride and arrogance, becomes genuinely humble and is able to cry out, "Oh God, I need help!" These are the three hardest words for a human being to utter: "I need help."

Lillian Roth's story of overcoming alcoholism is a poignant illustration. In her words: "I struggled with my drinking problem for years. I kept saying, 'I can handle my liquor.' I refused to accept the truth that I was an alcoholic. I procrastinated; I rationalized: 'Some day I will cut down. I can handle it.' It was not until I hit the bottom that I was able to admit defeat and then say the hardest words I ever uttered in my entire life, 'God, I need help!' "

Only when you reach those depths of despair are you then on the way to joy, because God particularly pours out His blessings upon those who know how much they need Him.

The promise is Joy, the principle is to ask God for help; admit you cannot do it alone. The problem, of course, that stands in the way of your crying out to God is the problem of an unholy pride. There is such a thing as a holy pride and an unholy pride. Self-respect and self-esteem is a proper and holy pride; arrogance and vanity is an improper and unholy pride. "Get out of my way, I want to do it myself." Like my son, when he was little, he did not want me or his mother to help him; he wanted to do it all by himself.

The principle is: Happiness comes when you surrender your arrogance and ask for help. Pride keeps us from crying out; greed also stops us. We want to take all the credit for our success.

I want to share with you one of the most valuable sentences I've ever read and one which I committed to memory long ago:

GOD CAN DO TREMENDOUS THINGS

THROUGH THE PERSON WHO DOES

NOT CARE WHO GETS THE CREDIT.

If you are willing to accept this basic premise, then you are willing to hire highly qualified people in your company or your corporation. They will make your business venture a success. They will get the credit.

This church is a living example of dynamic growth through the success of many. We have a Minister of Evangelism who has lay evangelists working on his team. We have a Minister of Education who has trained over 400 lay church teachers. We have a Minister of Family and Parish Life who works with a conscientious group of New Hope telephone counselors. Much of the credit for the success of the Garden Grove Community Church is duly given to the unselfish dedication of these fine people.

Poor in spirit? If you know you need help and if you know you cannot do it alone; and if you are willing to cry out to God and to people, God will bless you. What is your problem, my friend? What is blocking you from happiness? I can tell you this. Untold joy, gladness, even exultation will be yours when you realize that you must kneel before God Almighty. We are all poor in spirit. The Archbishop Fulton J. Sheen said to me, "The worst thing in the world is not the fact that people are sinners, but the worst thing in the world is, they are sinners and they won't admit it."

And so, we play our games, we put on our false fronts, and we join our clubs. We will do anything to try to avoid the one thing that is necessary, and that one thing is Repentance. We reach a point in life when we know that we are spiritually bankrupt. It is at this point where we finally will kneel before our Lord and say, "God, I want to be born again. I want a new life. I want a joyful Christ to come and live in me. At this moment in my life, Oh God, I make the total commitment. I turn my life over to you." This, my friends, is the pathway to carry out the principle of self-realization of sins, and thus to enjoy the promise of genuine joy and real happiness.

I invite you to look into yourselves, quietly, deliberately, thoroughly. Make your personal commitment to Jesus Christ today—now. You have tried so many other paths, traveled so many other roads, unsuccessfully. Why don't you try the obvious way—surrender your soul to the Savior; this is your manifest destiny. Kneel, and you will be knighted.

GOD FIRST;

OTHERS SECOND;

I AM THIRD.

CHAPTER TWO

Look at what you have left in life . . .
Never look at what you have lost!

"Blessed are those who mourn, for they
shall be comforted."

(Matt. 5:4)

2

How to Make a Comeback
from Heartbreak

If you have been walking through heartbreak valley, I have good news for YOU!

Jesus said it: "Blessed are those who mourn, for they shall be comforted. (Matt. 5:4) In the words of an old hymn: "Earth has no sorrow that Heaven cannot heal." *It is possible* for the vacant spot to be filled with a new love. *It is possible* for the smashed vase to be tenderly repaired and restored, or replaced. *It is possible* to make a comeback after heartbreak.

As a pastor I am in the specialized work of dealing with the hurt, the lonely, the suffering, the sick, the dying. For twenty years I have been trudging the soft, green lawns of cemeteries with my arms around young wives, husbands, fathers, mothers, relatives, and other loved ones. I have watched caskets lowered—hundreds of them: tiny ones, medium sized, and large ones—draped in flowers and flags, in a graduation gown, pulpit gown, and a bridal dress. Believe me, I am not blind to the reality of suffering. I have walked and wept my way through human sorrow. William Saroyan, who was recently interviewed on television, said, "Sorrow is a cloud which hangs over everyone, always in this life."

There are a vast number and variety of emotional experiences human beings undergo bearing the general label, "sorrow." Marie De Jong, a friend of mine and a member of Garden Grove Community Church, shared these intimate feelings with me upon the death of her husband: "No two sorrows are the same. I lost my son as a teenager; I lost my daughter in her twenties. Now my husband has passed away. Each grief has been painful; but each grief has been different." It is possible to be happy even in a world where sorrow casts its long, gray shadow. We have it on the best authority that "Blessed are those who mourn, for they shall be comforted." (Matt. 5:4)

HOW CAN YOU MAKE A COMEBACK AFTER HEARTBREAK?

I.
DO NOT BLAME GOD FOR THE SORROW

High in the mountains there is a spring which bubbles out of the rocks, tumbling down to form a crystal clear brook in the canyon valley. At its course, you can cup your hand and drink in the pure, clear, sparkling water. Two miles downstream you can see a rusty beer can bobbing along, leaving a rusty brown wake behind.

Ahead you watch as the occupant of a nearby cabin comes out his back door, walks over to the stream, and throws in a sack of garbage. By the time this stream becomes a river, it has also become a sewer. Who is to blame? Certainly it is not the fault of the spring high in the mountains!

God is the Spring and Source of Joy-Peace-Love. Never would God pollute the stream of humanity with the stain and spoil of sorrow. The supreme heresy is a wild idea which turns sincere believers into honest atheists. I'm referring to the ridiculous notion that somehow God sends suffering, sorrow, sickness, and death. The God of Christ creates only life, love, health, and wholeness. See for yourself; draw your own conclusion. Is it not true that sorrow, hurt, and heartache are *always* caused, directly or indirectly, innocently or intentionally, by imperfect people? This is the meaning of the Bible when it speaks of sin as the source of sorrow.

Visualize, please, the following headlines from newspapers:

GRANDSTAND COLLAPSES— DOZENS ARE KILLED

God's will? Ridiculous! Investigation of the accident reveals that a greedy promoter oversold the tickets and thereby overloaded the seating. Further investigation disclosed that a greedy contractor cut corners on necessary reinforcement in order to make more money for himself.

DAM GIVES WAY— MANY LIVES LOST

God's will? Blasphemy! Who, then, is at fault? Those human beings who ignorantly, or selfishly, failed to build and reinforce the dam properly in the beginning. Let's not wrongly blame God for the dam's giving way or the resultant suffering. A relative mourning the loss of a relative in such an accident said, "I warned him: 'It's dangerous living under that dam. You should move. Get out before it goes.' But he just laughed and said, 'I like it here. And, besides, I figure when my time is up, I'll go.'" If we ignore common sense, wise warnings, safety standards, then let's not blame God!

LUNG CANCER TAKES THE LIFE OF A YOUNG HUSBAND AND BELOVED FATHER

"Why would God take my husband? Why didn't God realize that life holds nothing for me without my husband!" the widow said to me. I had to answer, "Stop that thinking! Don't blame God! It was not He who invented, sold, or in any way encouraged your husband to smoke those cigarettes which the physician said could be the cause of cancer." Lay the blame where it belongs —squarely on the shoulders of imperfect people!

HEAD-ON COLLISION TAKES THE LIVES OF FOUR

Following a grinding, glass-splintering crash, there was only silence from the rubble in the ditch alongside the busy highway. Tens of thousands lose their lives in a similar manner. Never . . . never blame God. God gave us feet on which to walk; He did not invent the automobile. In all such accidents, investigate the causes and you will always find that men are at fault: rebellion against wearing seat belts, rebellion against speeding laws, rebellion against "Don't Drive when you Drink" rules.

Don't blame God for man-made accidents. I sincerely believe that God is not responsible for *one single* unfortunate event resulting from man's carelessness, unawareness, or ignorance. Investigate, interrogate, and then draw your own conclusion—human error is always the culprit: error of judgment, error of will, or error of purpose. Human selfishness, indifference, rebellion, folly, stupidity, brashness will always be found as the tap root cause of human misery and suffering.

CANCER AND HEART DISEASE— ALONG WITH OTHER RELATED ILLNESSES ARE THE TOP KILLERS IN AMERICA TODAY

No one will ever be able to place the blame for these diseases on God. In time, or in eternity, we shall see the truth: all disease is DISEASE—a lack of harmony between a human organism and its environment. Disease is too often caused by not eating right, not sleeping right, not exercising right, not breathing or breeding right—a question of man not attaining a harmonious balance with his surroundings. If disease appears, man is doing something wrong; God is not to blame!

I HEAR SOME QUESTIONS from my audience! I want to take this opportunity to answer two questions which are most often asked.

QUESTION ONE

Can't we blame God for not letting us know how these deaths could have been avoided or how these illness could have been cured?

Think a moment. The real problem is not our

ignorance, but our carelessness. Almost all disease, death, and sorrow is brought upon us, not through lack of knowledge, but through lack of obedience to the light God has given us. For instance:

1. God revealed the Ten Commandments. He gave us these ten laws to protect us from an alluring, tempting path which would ultimately lead only to sickness, sin, and sorrow. To follow the Ten Commandments will result in spiritual health, mental health, and physical health! Killing, lying, stealing, adultery, are bad for the health! (Consider the current epidemic of venereal diseases!) Under the banner of sophistication and liberation, many of us tell God to go to Hell! In so doing, we send only ourselves there.

2. God revealed secrets of health. He has given us fantastic insight into the sound condition of the body and the mind and its inherent wholeness. He has listed rules for us to follow regarding our daily bodily habits of eating, drinking, sleeping, working, exercising. Yet, is it not true that the doctor still smokes and drinks to an excess, and that the minister eats improperly, fails to exercise often enough, and generally overlooks his physical well-being? Can we honestly and fairly accuse God for not giving us more insight into health when we blatantly disregard the knowledge he has revealed?

3. God disclosed secrets of salvation from sin.

We know that sorrow, separation, sickness and disease are caused by sin. To illustrate, we know that physical illness is caused by mental tension, stress, worry, anxiety, fear, and guilt. We also know that if we accept salvation and yield our minds and our hearts to the *Saving Spirit of Christ*, our negative sins and emotions will be drawn out and healing of mind and body will follow. Yet, many of us are still hesitant to give ourselves over completely to Christ; thus we reject God's salvation. "How shall we escape if we neglect such a great salvation?" (Heb. 2:3)

Remember the key to happiness:

GOD FIRST—others second;

I'm Third

QUESTION TWO

Can we not blame God for permitting people to be so selfish? Doesn't God have the almighty power to control every person on earth, to force each one to obey Him, to make no mistakes, and to commit no sins?

IF God had the power to so manipulate and dominate the lives of all persons on earth in order to remove all human causes of sorrow; namely, rebellion, selfishness, and ignorance; would it not stand to reason that God would also be responsible for NOT purging and purifying the world? Think on this a moment or two. We might even go further in our thinking and blame God for creating man with the capability toward sin. But remember the dilemmas that faced God at the dawn of creation. God wanted to make a materialized form of life which would be a reflection of His own non-materialized Self. Thus, He chose to make Man "after his image." So, God designed man to be a decision-making creature, capable of discernment, judgment, evaluation, choice, and decision.

When God created such a Man, He realized fully that this creature would have the power to decide against God. But, let's look at the alternative left to God. If He designed a Man who could never make a wrong decision, this would mean that God must constantly be pouring information into this creature. How horrible! This creature would be absolutely UNABLE to make a personal decision of his own. He would be nothing but a glorified computer—a PERFECT, sinless, guiltless, error-less . . . person? NO! Machine? Yes! Computer? Yes! Human being . . . NEVER!

God decided to take the greatest gamble of the ages—to make an opinion-forming, idea-collecting, decision-making creature, for above all else, God is love; therefore, any creature made in His image would have to be a loving creature. And only a free-will creature can love. For, IF love is programmed and manipulated, it is not love; it is only an echo of the programmer! *Real love* is possible only from a person with the free will to choose.

If you are "controlled" to love another because of an order, or a command, or through manipulation, then you are not experiencing love; you are merely a recorder replaying the input of someone else. If I love you because I am designed ONLY to love, what honor is that to you? But if I love you—and you know that I have freely chosen not to ignore and abandon you . . . or reject you . . . but I have chosen to love you, then love is truly real, authentic, sincere, and self-esteem boosting.

So God, in His hour of decision, at the dawn of creation, realized He could have created human beings incapable of sin. BUT, to do this would be to create puppets, not people. What is wrong with that, if the results are good? You'd have sinless but non-loving persons.

Understand this:

> *A perfect world is not simply a world*
>   *without sin:*
> *A perfect world is a world EMPTY of sin*
>   *and FILLED with love!*
>
> *A perfect field is not simply a farm free*
>   *of weeds:*
> *A perfect field is a farm free of weeds*
>   *and covered with vegetable and fruit-bearing*
>   *plants!*

So, God took the big gamble and created a free-will potential sinner, but potentially loving person called Man.

Don't *blame* God for permitting sin. *Thank* God that He has never, in spite of our sins, taken our freedom from us and with it, our capability of becoming sincere, loving persons.

Don't blame God for the suffering in this world! Blame man for personally choosing the path leading to heartache and sorrow. Blame man for rejecting the divine truth when it was shown to him. Blame man for refusing God's salvation, even when offered in the name of Jesus!

For God so loved the world, that he gave his only begotten Son, that whosoever believeth in him should not perish, but have everlasting life. (John 3:16)

If, after man sinned, God had let him go to Hell without trying to save him, then, perhaps, you could blame God for not offering a second chance. You have but to look at the cross and know that no man can ever blame God for going the limit to save man.

HOW CAN YOU MAKE A COMEBACK AFTER HEARTBREAK?

II.
DO NOT BLAME YOURSELF!

Guilt always seems to be associated with grief. Self-condemnation will solve no problem and will change no circumstance. It is merely a negative, non-constructive emotion. A member of our church showed me a slogan used by the company where she works:

DON'T FIX THE BLAME,
FIX THE PROBLEM!

What is your problem? First, recognize that the *real* problem is not the death of a loved one. This is unchangeable. The real problem is *your reaction to this fact.*

How do you "fix the problem"?

(1) Decide not to go on for the rest of your life surrendering to sorrow and tears. To do this only disgraces your loved ones, your friends, and yourself. Moreover, continued grief *dishonors the God who wants only to be credited with giving you a rebirth of joy!* Decide that this non-constructive sorrow mixed with self-pity has got to STOP!

(2) *Do not accept defeat.* "The death thy death hath dealt to me, is worse than the death thy death hath dealt to thee!" These words were spoken by a widow in a Greek tragedy as she stood looking at the body of her dead husband. Do not quit! When the going gets tough, the tough get going! Be brave! Fight back! Come back again. There is a world out there—hungry, hurting. Think of them; they are alive; they need you!

In the book, "Gone With the Wind," we read about the southern gentleman who broke down under the tragedies involved in the Civil War. Observing his collapse, another character in the novel philosophizes: "He could be licked from the inside. I mean to say that what the world could not do, his own heart could." Then the simple philosopher concluded: "There ain't anything from the outside that can lick any of us."

(3) *Bury your selfish griefs.* Grief which keeps you from thinking of and helping others is selfish. Around you is a world filled with living human beings who are hurting more than you are hurting. There are lonely, heartbroken, dying women—men—children out here! They need you. You are stronger than they are. You can comfort them.

The secret of happiness that is reiterated throughout the Beatitudes can be summed up in two words: "I'm third." If it applies in the first Beatitude, it also applies in the second Beatitude. Are you hurting? How do you come back alive again? Think of God first; think of others second; and then put yourself third. And if you are so withdrawn into your own world of loneliness and grief that you don't care if others are hurting, then you are too self-centered!

(4) *Add up your joys; never count your sorrows.* Look at what you have left in life; never look at what you have lost. At a time of sorrow you are so overwhelmed and swamped by the shock, the pain, and the grief, that you are not even conscious of the joys that still are alive deep under that blanket of grief. Determine to uncover

your smothered joys and let them breathe and
flourish again! There are many things that you
are still thankful for even though you do not feel
your gratitude. Now begin by reminiscing. Relive
your happy memories. Treat yourself to a play-
back of that great collection or joyful experiences
that have occurred in your past. There are many
wonderful things that have happened to you in
life. Pause a moment to think of your childhood;
recall some childhood experiences. Move on
through life and make a disciplined, determined,
dedicated effort to recall, and then relish for a
few moments the happy times. Give yourself a
delightful, emotional feast on pleasant recollec-
tions. After a while, you will discover there is still
much that you can be joyful about.

I have a friend who keeps an "Italian
philosophy" poem on his restaurant wall. The
restaurant is Mr. Angelo's and is located in Garden Grove, California. The following are the
words, worth remembering:

> *Count your garden by the flowers;*
>   *Never by the leaves that fall.*
> *Count your days by golden hours;*
>   *Don't remember clouds at all.*
> *Count your nights by stars, not shadows;*
>   *Count your life with smiles, not tears.*
> *And with joy on every birthday,*
>   *Count your age by friends, not years!*

(5) *Turn your sorrow into a servant.* If you
have buried your selfish griefs, you are ready to

turn your sorrow into a helpful partner. Grief can be a demonic dictator if you will let it. It can turn you into a cynical, doubting, resentful, self-pitying recluse or drunkard. Sorrow never leaves you where it found you. It will change you—into a better person or into a worse person. It will drive you closer to God or it will drive you so far from God that you will never want to believe in Him again. You will make the choice! You will choose how you will react. Do not let sorrow become a devil that will drive you. Let it become a servant that will serve God, your fellow man, and as a result, sorrow will serve you the greatest feast of joy that you have ever known! If sorrow will turn you into a mellow, gentle, tender, compassionate soul, it will serve you well indeed.

"IN LOVE'S SERVICE, ONLY BROKEN HEARTS WILL DO."

I recently received a letter from a listener of the Hour of Power in New York. I have read and re-read the letter so often that I know it almost by memory. Let me share it with you:

"Dear Dr. Schuller: I have never written a letter like this before in my life. This is the story of a bitter man—and the person who saved him. I am the bitter man. In 1961, I was married. I loved my wife. We still love each other very much. It is the only thing that has kept me going. Shortly after our marriage we suffered a financial reverse. This really made me bitter. Then we wanted children and discovered we could have

none. This made me more bitter. After a while
we adopted a child and for a brief time we were
very happy. Then we discovered that this adopted
child, a little boy we named Joey, was mentally
retarded from brain damage! That made me bitter. But the bitterest day in my life was in May,
1971. Little Joey died. When we buried him, I
was so bitter; I didn't believe in God, Christ, or
anybody or anything.

For some months now my wife has been watching this religious television program on Sunday
mornings. She begged me to watch with her; but
I wouldn't. Six weeks ago, I happened to walk
through the living room when something you said
caught my attention. I listened. I listened to
everything. I listened the next week, and the next,
and the next week. I am writing to tell you that
in six short weeks I am now a changed person.
All my bitterness is gone. And I am thanking you
because you introduced me to Jesus Christ. Because of this, my wife and I decided to dedicate
our lives to helping mentally retarded children. I
can't tell you what a changed life I have because
my thinking has changed through Christ. Joyfully
yours, An Hour of Power Listener.''

Let your sorrow turn you into a better person
and your sorrow will turn out to be a blessing!

(6) *Accept the comfort God is trying to offer
you.* At the beginning of this chapter, I said that
God is not the source of sorrow. Man brought
sorrow and man continues to bring sorrow into
this world. God moves in immediately and forth-

rightly to bring comfort. He offers the comfort of His promises of love and eternal life.

A friend of mine back East saw her only two children killed as teenagers in tragic accidents. "How could you come back again after losing your last child?" I asked her. She answered, "Somebody sent me a letter that said, 'Through all this tragedy never forget these words: God still loves you.' Those words were words that I clung to; and they saved me!" She smiled as she said it. Accept God's presence; accept God's promises; accept God's pardon for your own sin and guilt. You will then enjoy His promises of eternal life! That means that you have not seen the last of the loved one who moved on ahead of you!

Albert Einstein has presented theories which modern sound engineers have taken up. We are now told that sound waves never die. Sound waves generated by Abraham Lincoln at Gettysburg, the sound waves generated by Jesus Christ when He uttered the Sermon on the Mount; these sound waves are still alive and vibrating in this universe!

Now for the unbelievable! I was told by a leading expert that predictions are that the day will come when these sound waves will be sorted out, recalled, and recorded, and then played back so that we can actually hear the voices as spoken years and centuries ago! You say that it is crazy! I agree with you! As a young boy, I also said that it was crazy when they told me that man would someday walk on the moon and we on planet earth would be able to watch him and hear him at the same time!

Sound waves do not die. Souls that pass on do not die! They are alive out there! Jesus knew this. He tried to communicate it to us when He said, "Whoever lives and believes in me shall never die." (Jn. 11:26) "In my Father's house are many rooms; if it were not so, would I have told you that I go to prepare a place for you?" (Jn. 14:2) Because of this, we have the assurance, the good news, that eternal life is offered to you today.

Accept this comfort that God offers to you. Remember that God's comfort is not a cushion to keep you down and nurse your tears. God's comfort is not a weakening sympathy to feed your self-pity. God's comfort is the Holy Spirit. Jesus said, "And he shall give you another Comforter, that he may abide with you for ever." (Jn. 14:16) What is this comforting Holy Spirit? It is the spirit of God which comes to inspire you with courage, with new enthusiasm for life, with a dream, with an inner ear which will cause you to hear the cry of a suffering child who calls to you in the night! Respond to this Spirit within you now. Someone needs you. Turn around. Look behind you. Offer a hand; offer a heart. Some child will smile because you cared.

You will have discovered that

   YOU have made a

     COMEBACK from heartbreak.

CHAPTER THREE

Happy are those who put Jesus First, Others Second, and place themselves Third!

"Blessed are the meek, for they shall inherit the earth."

(Matt. 5:5)

3

How to Win the World Around You

"BLESSED ARE THE MEEK, for they shall inherit the earth!"

Doesn't that sound ridiculous? We live in a high-powered, dynamic, energetic, promotional country called the United States of America.

Don't we all know that it is the high-energy, powerful promoter, big wheeler-dealer that gets ahead? "Blessed are the meek, for they shall inherit the earth." (Matt. 5:5) If Jesus had said, "Blessed are the meek, for theirs is the kingdom of heaven," that we could understand. But when He said, "Blessed are the meek, for they shall inherit the earth," it sounds like a gross statement of ridicule. Until you study the Greek origin of the word "blessed," you can not really understand what that word means. I am not going to give you a lesson in Greek; but I did translate that Beatitude in several other ways to clarify its meaning.

Blessed are the Patient: They shall *overcome* their problems and *work through* their difficulties. They shall preserve their family and friends. They shall gain ground, acquire an education, save money, build lasting relationships, lay solid foundations, and will truly succeed in the business of living life on this earth! Blessed are the Patient: They shall inherit the earth's highest achievements!

Blessed are the Emotionally controlled: They shall hold their tongues. They shall tame their wild tempers. They shall develop a disciplined divine poise. They shall hold in check their negative impulses. They shall avoid and resist distractions and temptations which would excite and stimulate, but drain their financial, moral, and physical resources. Blessed are the Emotionally Controlled. They will make successes of their lives on this earth.

Blessed are the honest, hard-working folks: They are more interested in substance than in style. They are more concerned about character building than popularity rating. They are more dedicated to making solid achievements than to making fast, but phony happiness. They are quick to pass on the credit to others. Blessed are they, for they shall be loved and respected by good people in this life!

Blessed are the teachable: They shall learn much before it is too late. Blessed are those who know what it is that they do not know, and are eager to listen to older, wiser, and more experienced seers. Blessed indeed are they who, in true meekness, remember that a little learning is a dangerous thing. Blessed are those who never forget that they are never too old to learn. Blessed are they, for they shall inherit great wisdom and, with it, success!

Blessed are the sensitive spirits: They shall inherit the affection of all good people. Happy indeed is the heart which is sensitive to another's *insecurity*. Loving is he who offers reassurance to another's *hostility*, affection to another's *loneliness*, friendship to another's *hurt*, and apologies to all. Blessed are such sensitive souls, for they shall inherit the devotion and esteem of good people on this earth!

Blessed are the powerful people: They have learned to restrain their power. They know that the real power is in its control and discipline lest it rip out young plants with the uprooting of the weeds, and tear out the tender plants of human kindness and gentleness. Yes, blessed are those who remain gentle while they build strength, who are merciful while they are mighty. Blessed are they, for they shall not merely win a war, they shall win the hearts of a nation!

Blessed are the Quiet people: They do so much good for so many without fanfare, glory-seeking or headline-hunting. They shall inherit the trust, respect, and love of the truly beautiful people on this earth!

Blessed are the truly Creative persons: They turn their problems into projects, their sorrows into servants, their difficulties into dividends, their obstacles into opportunities, their tragedies into triumphs, their stumbling blocks into stepping stones. They look upon an interruption as an interesting interlude. They harvest fruit from frustration. They convert enemies into friends! They look upon adversities as adventures. Blessed are they, for they shall inherit self-respect in their life!

Blessed are the truly humble: They shall seek truth. Knowing they lost it, they shall surely find it. They shall accept criticism, knowing that they are not perfect. They shall yield the floor to those who are better informed. They shall be big enough to say, "I'm sorry," and "I am wrong." Happy are the humble-hearted, for they shall receive forgiveness from their God and their fellow man! They shall receive peace of mind on this earth!

Blessed are those who are willing to be third: Happy are those who put Jesus first, others second, and place themselves third in line. Richly rewarded in this life are those who learn the lesson of our Lord that if any man would be a master, let him also be a servant. "If any one would be first, he must be last of all and servant of all." (Mark 9:35) "For whoever would save his life will lose it; and whoever loses his life for my sake, he will save it." (Luke 9:24) Blessed are they, for they shall inherit a beautiful life on this earth!

Blessed are the God-shaped, Christ-molded people:

I received a marvelous picture from Bishop Fulton Sheen, inscribed, "To my dear friend Dr. Robert Schuller"; and then this text:

> "Some come in Chariots,
>
> Some on horses,
>
> But we come in the name of the Lord."

Yes, blessed are those humble people who come not with a big splash and a lot of show, but who honestly come carrying the word of the Lord. It begins to make sense, doesn't it?

"Blessed are the meek, for they shall inherit the earth." (Matt. 5:5)

Of course! Consider it by its contrast. *Cursed*

is the cocky, arrogant, haughty, boastful under-dog: for he will have few friends! *Unhappy is the elbowing,* crowding, shoving, pushing, get-out-of-my-way-I'm-first bully: for he shall make many enemies! *Headed for sure failure* is the know-it-all Joe. Get out of my way. I want to do it my way. Deaf to constructive criticism, careless of shrewd counsel, and indifferent to warnings, he is headed for a fall!

Doomed is the hot-head! Pride and uncontrolled temper come before the fall. Unhappy is the man who loses his cool and is too proud to say, "I'm sorry." He will never inherit the earth. He will not even hold his job, or perhaps his wife. Hell-bent on this earth are the impatient, restless, rootless, ruthless promoters. They may gain a crown and lose the Kingdom! What shall it profit a man if he gains the world and loses his own soul?

The Beatitude begins to sound like the best advice ever offered for happy living: "Blessed are the meek, for they shall inherit the earth."

Indeed it is true. In the long pull those who win the world around them are those whom Jesus calls the meek, the controlled, the patient, the honest, the quiet, the forceful, the powerful-but restrained, disciplined, poised person. He is God-molded, Christ-shaped, Spirit-dominated.

Blessed are the meek, for they shall inherit the earth." Who are they? I met a number of them, about 185, in a school recently in Long Beach, California. The Florence Nightingale School is a part of the public school system. It is for the mentally retarded. The principal, Clyde Thompson, and Larry Bruns, a member of the staff, are members of my congregation. They invited us to visit the school. It was an unforgettable experience.

The mentally retarded fall into three classifications. In the highest classification are the educable. They can earn a high school diploma. They can go out into society and most people will never know that they are mentally retarded.

In the lowest classification are those who are incapable of any education—the hydra-headed, the huge-headed children; and the micro-headed, the tiny-headed children. In between is the mass group for whom they have schools. They are the mongoloid, the Down syndrome children, and many others. They are not able to learn to read; they are not able to learn to count; but they do understand pictures. A picture that reads "EXIT" to you, is to them a picture which means that this is the way to get out. "WARNING" spells warning to you; but to them it is a picture which means to be careful. The words, "Do Not Cross the Street," mean something specific to you; to them it means "Do not walk across the street where you see this picture."

We went through this school and it was fantastic. Every person in the school from the age of six through twenty-one years learns to do things creatively. I bet twenty kids stopped Mr. Thompson as Mrs. Schuller and I were walking with him. They would run up to him and say, "Mr. Thompson, look—I did it all by myself." Over and over, we heard this same sentence.

"Blessed are the meek, for they shall inherit joy on this earth." Love on this earth. Happiness on this earth. I want to say something here, because many people in today's modern society are still woefully ignorant about these mentally retarded. First, they are harmless. In the Florence Nightingale School they record no problems of violence, street fighting, knifing, or kicking. These children are lovable. You do not see scribbling on the walls. You do not see graffiti; you do not see scratches on desks. They just do not have this. If somebody loses a pencil or a coin on the playground, the first child who finds it will run to the principal's office and say, "Here, I found this on the grass." There is no stealing. They are beautiful people.

Everyone learns to do something; nobody fails in that school. They are taught to be creative: to weave, to sew, to print, or to draw. When they finish school, there is a factory down the street where they are all hired and can work. I watched as they filled an order for a commercial firm which made garden hoses. They needed to put six washers in a little plastic bag. It was set up like an assembly line. All the graduates of the school were doing this. How can they make sure they get only six washers in the plastic bag? Very simply. The educators have developed a little piece of

wood which is about one inch high. The children
are told to put enough washers on that wood to
reach the top. When this happens, they empty the
washers into the plastic bag. It takes just six
washers. They never make a mistake. They work
a full day; they do not complain. They are happy
and they are beautiful persons.

I left that school surrounded by a mental environment of love, good-will, creativity, and self-
esteem: "I did it all by myself!" We got onto the
Garden Grove Freeway, going home, and some
bully in a big car almost ran me onto the shoulder, tooting his horn. I looked at my wife and
said, "Who are the mentally retarded?" "Blessed
are the meek, for they shall inherit the earth."

Rosie Gray was buried in a simple ceremony in
a cemetery in the little town of El Toro years
ago. We started this church in a drive-in theater
for want of a better place. We built a little chapel
on the roof of the drive-in. At this time I was
asked to baptize a woman who could not walk
and could not talk. Her husband lifted her into
their car and drove her to the drive-in every Sunday. Her name was Rosie Gray.

I will never forget Warren Gray, her husband,
meeting me outside his little ranch house one day
and saying, "Reverend Schuller, before you meet
my wife I must tell you something about her.
You might think she does not have her senses,
but her mind is perfect, absolutely perfect. She
had a stroke and she cannot raise her head. She
cannot close her eyes and she cannot move them.

They simply stare ahead. Her head just stays on her chest. She cannot walk; she cannot talk. She can cry a little and grunt a little, but that is all."

I went into the house, and I can still see her sitting there. I called there dozens of times in the next five years. She always sat in the same chair, her head resting with her chin on her chest, eyes always open, never blinking, motionless, as if she were made out of plastic. I said, "Rosie, do you love Jesus?" A tear formed and rolled down her cheek. "Rosie, do you want to be baptized?" A couple more tears rolled down and she grunted, "Ugh, Ugh, Ughh, Uggh." The following Sunday they parked their car in the front row of the drive-in. I had a long dropcord on my microphone, and I walked down and baptized her in her car. At that time we were ready to move into the beautiful chapel that we had just built on two acres of land. What are we going to do about Rosie Gray now?

The decision was made to have services at 9:30 in the new chapel and I was to go to the drive-in as long as Rosie lived. "That won't be long," they said. But she lived one year, two years, three years, four years, five years—she just would not die. Amazing! Finally, God put the dream for this present church in our minds; it was His dream. We bought the land, and we had the groundbreaking ceremony on a Sunday. The local newspapers ran the story on Monday—the ground had been broken for what was to be the world's first walk-in, drive-in church. The story came out on Monday morning, and on Monday afternoon I had a funeral . . . for Rosie Gray.

I shall always remember that this church would not be here if it had not been for Rosie Gray.

Blessed are the meek: for they will make a new impact on this earth far beyond what they themselves know.

Jesus Christ proved it, above all. He was led like a lamb to the slaughter—despised, rejected of men. A man of sorrows who was acquainted with grief. Pilate thought he had won; Herod was sure that Jesus had lost; everybody was convinced this fellow was wiped out for good. Today who is alive? Jesus Christ is alive. Pilate is dead.

"Blessed are the meek, for they shall inherit the earth!"

Give God time and it will always work out this way.

Now—look at the ultimate example of the truly "Meek"—look at Jesus Christ.

He was controlled emotionally
   —spat upon,
     insulted,
       stripped,
         ridiculed,
           despised, He was
  led as a Lamb to the Slaughter.
YET HE NEVER STRUCK BACK!
  Foolish?
  He inherited the earth,
  didn't He? There's not

a land where He is
not loved!

He demonstrated quiet determination:
Steadfastly, He set His face to Jerusalem.
He knew what He had to do. He did it!
A Sacrifice on the Cross!

RIDICULOUS? INSANE?
He inherited the earth,
didn't He? Men of every
color and motivational origin
kneel before Him!

He was Gentle, Kind, Forgiving, Loving
even to those who killed Him.
STUPID, YOU SAY? WAS IT?
He could face God with a clear conscience
when He died!
"It is finished," He said. And today
The World Loves Him!

His enemies? They are the truly dead. Pilate, who used power without love, lives on in infamy. "Suffered under Pontius Pilate" is a phrase repeated by millions of churches in the Apostles' Creed.

But Christ lives on!

I remember the lines of a great poet who said:

I saw the conquerors riding by
With cruel lip and faces wan.
Musing on empires sacked and burned
There rode the Mongol Genghis Khan.

And Alexander like a God
Who sought to weld the world in one
And Caesar with his laurel wreath
And like a thing from hell—the Hun.

And leading like a star—the van
Heedless of upstretched arm and groan,
Inscrutable Napoleon rode
Dreaming of empire and alone.

But they all perished from the scene
Like fleeting shadows on a glass
And conquering down the centuries
Comes Christ the Swordless on an ass.

"Blessed are the meek, for they shall inherit the earth!" (Matt. 5:5)

CHAPTER FOUR

It's better to do something imperfectly
Than to do nothing perfectly!

"Blessed are those who hunger and thirst for righteousness, for they shall be satisfied."

(Matt. 5:6)

4

How to Satisfy Your Heart's Restless Passion

I received a letter recently from a lovely young teenager. She writes:

"The Sermon on the Mount was wonderful. It really changed my whole attitude toward life. My Mom tells me to do the dishes and be a nice kid. I always complain and yell at her; but tonight I didn't. I surprised her and I said, 'Okay.' It was the shock of the century. When I was listening to the sermon and watching you, tears rolled down my face. I finally realized how selfish I was before, and what a snotty teenager I was. It is all different now. Am I happy! I smile. I even help my Mom! I was so happy, I was smiling in the shower washing my hair. Thank you so very much, Reverend Schuller, because I really learned how to pray now without being afraid that somebody would catch me on my knees by my bed. I even quit yelling at my younger sister. Thank you so very much. Your special friend . . ."

Here's a young girl who has discovered the key to happiness. Now it's your turn!

People are changing all the time. You are changing. You will change as you read these words . . . particularly, if you can learn to say two words, "Yes, Lord." Let me explain something. In such a negative-thinking world, we are constantly surrounded by many negative vibrations. The most positive person you meet still has his negative attitudes. No person is one hundred percent positive. We are emotionally conditioned to negativity by the world in which we live. So our first inclination toward many positive suggestions is to say, "No." How do we break these hypnotizing, negative chains? How do we liberate ourselves? There are people who talk about Women's Lib; I am for self-lib.

How do you liberate yourself from the imprisonment of negative thinking? One way to begin is to speak positive affirmations out loud. It is a dynamic, healing, mind-changing exercise. It is positive; it is not going to hurt you. Right now, lay this book on your lap and say the words, "Yes, Lord." Repeat them out loud until they sound natural.

"YES, LORD; YES, LORD."

Do not be afraid of seeming to be overly dramatic, or of being overly emotional; do not let any negative fear hold you back. Say it strongly, positively, "Yes, Lord." I predict that within an hour a positive thought will come into your mind. A positive mood will begin to creep over you. When that happens do not say, "No"; say, "Yes, Lord."

Perhaps it is an invitation to turn your life over to Christ. There are those of you who have never yet made a commitment of your life to Jesus Christ, accepting Him as your Savior and your Lord, your personal, living friend. I invite you to do so! If you have not committed your life to Christ, take this positive step today. It is obviously going to turn you into a better person, not a worse person. That makes it positive. So you say, "Yes, Lord"; not, "No, Lord."

There are three reasons, I believe, why people

would say "no" to God. Let's look at them. You
ask, "Why would any human being, unless he is
totally insane, ever say 'no' to God?" It is in-
comprehensible that a human being would say
"no" to a good idea. Yet people are doing it all
the time. Let us suppose that God is inspiring
you to drop a habit, an action which would make
you into a better person, and you say, "No,
God." God is calling you to be somebody that
He can use, and yet you have an inclination to
say, "No, God." Now, that is utter insanity—
when you think of it. Why do people say "no"
to God? I suggest three reasons.

*First, people say "no" to God because they do
not know any better.* There are still a lot of people who are hung up on the idea that if you really
get religion, and really get converted, and really
get saved or become a Christian, that you may go
off the deep end and become a little nutty, or
kooky, or freaky. So they steer away from religion. They just do not know any better. If they
only realized it, when they go the whole way,
they really have it.

Dwight Moody used to say, "People have just
enough religion to make themselves miserable:
they cannot be happy at a drinking party and
they are uncomfortable at a prayer meeting."

How true it is—many people have just enough
religion to be miserable. Get enough to enjoy it!
Some people say "no" to God because they do
not know any better. I do not blame them. The
only impression some people have of God is what

they have received from some hypocrites. No wonder they turn Him off!

There is a second reason why some people say "no" to God. It is because they do not think they can say "yes" to Him. Their thinking is: He is perfect and I surely know I am not; therefore, I do not think I should join up with Him. God does not call you to be perfect; He just calls you to be willing, that is all. You can say, "Lord, I am willing to try." God doesn't expect you to be sinless, but He does expect you to try to become sinless. Better to do something constructive imperfectly, than to do nothing perfectly.

Thirdly, some people say "no" to God because they think they are not quite ready. There are, they think, more important things on their minds. They have projects that they have not started; projects that are half-finished; telephone calls to make; unanswered letters to write. When they get their desks cleared and have a chance to think, probably only then will they turn to God; but right now they are just too busy. The trouble is, there may not be a "later on." Do it now! Do not let God wait. If you feel a positive, inspiring thought go through your mind today, there is only one way to answer it, "Yes, Lord!"

"Blessed are those who hunger and thirst for righteousness, for they shall be satisfied." What does this Beatitude mean? It means that the man who is really going to be satisfied, who really is going to feel as if he has succeeded in life in the business of living, is the person who has a passion to say "yes" to good ideas and stops saying "no" to great opportunities.

Now, to *live* this Beatitude, I am going to teach you three positive affirmations. There are three sentences I want you to learn to say:

(1) Yes, Lord, I should.

(2) Yes, Lord, I can.

(3) Yes, Lord, I will.

I.

Let's look at the first sentence: "Yes, Lord, I should." If a positive idea comes into your mind, ask yourself, "Would this be a great thing for God? Would it help people who are hurting? Would it make me into a better husband or a sweeter wife, or a better father or mother? Would it make me into a better child? Would it make me into a more beautiful person?" If this is true, say, "Yes, Lord, I should."

If there is some habit you should break—one you should start!—if there is some job you should do, or some dream you should go after, you simply ask, "Would it make me or my world into a better person or a better place?" If the answer is affirmative, then say, "Yes, Lord, I should." You don't ask, "Do I want to do it? Would it be fun? Would it be cheap? Would it be safe? Would it cost a lot?" This is not the important question—the important question is, "Would it make me into a better person?" In this there is the element of risk, but there is no progress without risk. Never!

Algetha Brown sings in the G.G.C.C. church, and participates in the Institutes for Successful Church Leadership. She is great. She is married to a career man in the Air Force, George Brown. After World War II they were stationed in Germany. This was during the time of the arrests and trials of war criminals at Neurenberg. There were innocent people who were being considered guilty due to their association with authentic criminals. Algetha and her husband tell about meeting some Germans who were hiding out because they were afraid they might be implicated in war crimes.

This was the setting. The scene begins at home where the oldest of their two sons was confined with the mumps. Their house was a fourth floor apartment. The boy was feeling pretty good, so he opened the window and sat on the window ledge, looking out on the world. A gust of wind came rushing through the house, closing the shutter violently. The boy lost his balance, fell to the cobblestoned street, but as he did so he ripped off an ornamental iron railing that cracked the window of the apartment two floors below. There were screams and calls for help, and soon there was the wail of an ambulance. The mother ordered the German ambulance driver to take the boy to the nearest hospital, the closest emergency room being in a civilian hospital.

Since Mr. Brown was in the Air Force, the American military doctors were called immediately. They came and examined the boy. One doctor said, "Your son has four compound fractures of the right arm, and it must be amputated. But, Mrs. Brown, thank God, he will live. From what we can tell there are no internal injuries and that is a miracle. We will go ahead and schedule the surgery."

After the doctors left, Mrs. Brown stood weeping softly at the unconscious boy's side. A German nurse who spoke English came up and said, "I probably should not say this, Mrs. Brown, but I know a German doctor who is brilliant. I think maybe he might be able to save your son's arm. But I do not think he would come to see you." Algetha lifted her head; questioningly, she asked, "Why? Because I am a Negro? Because my boy is black?" The German nurse stammered, "Oh no, no, it is not that, Mrs. Brown. It is just that this doctor is a German, and he had friends—you see—the wrong friends! He is afraid that if he comes out of hiding, he may be arrested and implicated in the war-crime trials. But, I will talk to him. He is not practicing now."

The next day the nurse came back and said, "Algetha, I talked to him. He is coming!" Later that night the doctor came in unnoticed. He approached the bed and checked the little boy's arm. "Mrs. Brown," he said, "that arm can be saved. It does not have to be amputated. I could do it. It would take seven operations to remove that many bone chips." Mrs. Brown said, "Would you, doctor?" He looked at her attentively, and then walked out of the room.

The next day in the hospital, as preparations were being finalized for the amputation, Mrs. Brown sat stoically by her son's bed. The nurse came in and said, "Mrs. Brown, the doctor called and he says he will do it! He will take the chance!" The doctor came out of hiding, performed the necessary seven operations, and saved the arm. The story of the doctor's medical feat leaked out and the result was arrest, a trial and a sentence to five years in prison. Today, thanks to that doctor's sacrifice, Algetha's boy's arm is almost like new.

After it was all over, Mrs. Brown said to the doctor, "Why did you do it, doctor? Why did you take the chance?" His answer was obvious! That German doctor *knew* he *should*! The boy was very grateful for that doctor's faith and ability. He said to his mother, "Mom, I am indebted to any man who thought enough of my arm to sentence himself to five years in prison. Because of this debt of gratitude, God has my hand and God has my arm for as long as He wants it. I am going to use it with His help, and I am going to make it into a doctor's hand, with a doctor's fingers, and pay that man back for the five years he gave for me." Today, that boy is a brilliant pre-medical student at the University of Colorado.

The question is not, "Do I want to? Would it be safe? Would it cost a lot?" The question is, "What is the right thing to do?" Learn to say the words, "Yes, Lord, I should."

II.

The second sentence that will make this Beatitude come alive is, "Yes, Lord, I can." If it is a good idea and you do not think you are able to do it, what do you do? Try it, anyway! Just because you lack talent, ability, or training, does not give you the right to say "no" to a good idea. It means you give God a chance to perform a miracle.

I went through the mid-West recently and I stopped in Mitchell, South Dakota, to visit a friend, Mrs. Tess, who teaches the mentally retarded in the public schools. She said she has used my "Move Ahead with Possibility Thinking" book for all the mentally retarded students in Mitchell. One room at the school is called, "The Possibility Room." Mrs. Tess wanted me to see what these children had learned. She had all the boys and girls stand up. Then they read out loud a long poem which was written on the board. I want to share it with you:

I don't like "don't."
I don't, I don't.
I hear a million times a day
No matter what I do they say.

   Now, don't do this and don't do that,
   Don't interrupt, don't tease the cat;
   Don't bite your nails, don't slam the door,
   Don't leave those messes on the floor.

Don't shout, don't fight, don't spill your food,
Don't talk back and don't be rude.
Don't let the dog climb on your bed
And don't forget what I just said.

Don't track in mud, don't slip, don't run,
Don't lose your cap, don't point your gun.
Don't touch the tray, don't tear your clothes,
Don't forget to blow your nose.

Don't go too far, don't climb that tree
And don't fall down and skin your knee.
I don't like "don't" one little bit,
Ah, now look, they've got me saying it.

That was only one example of Possibility Thinking becoming a reality. Incredible! Then Mrs. Tess had a little girl stand up and read another poem for me. She did it very well. Mrs. Tess whispered, "Doctor Schuller, that little girl who is reading can also write what she reads. She has an I.Q. of only 49." Now, believe me, I would have said, "That is impossible." I said to Mrs. Tess, "How can it be?" "Well," she said, "it does take a lot of time and a lot of work, but that little girl learns because she does not know that she cannot learn."

If an idea is a good idea, then somehow it can be done! Affirm out loud, "Yes, Lord, I should. Yes, Lord, I can."

I spoke to some people at a rally recently. One man wanted to meet me because he had seen me on television. He had no arms. There was nothing on the left side and just a stump on the right and a piece of steel clamp attached. "What happened?" I inquired, looking at the absence of arms. Before he had a chance to answer, I said, "Did you get it caught in a corn-picker?" "No," he said, "worse than that; I got it caught in a stone crusher down in the mine." He continued, "The machine pulled the whole left arm out by the shoulder socket. And my right arm got pulled off at the elbow. But that is all right! You would not believe what I can do, Reverend, with this one steel clamp! I can drive the car; I can dress myself; I can help in the kitchen; I can do most anything."

I listened to him as he kept saying, "*I can* do this; *I can* do this; *I can* do this; *I can* do this; *I can* do this." He was a great big, burly guy; he weighed close to 250 pounds! He was tough-looking. All of a sudden he got wet-eyed and said, "You know, that is why I had to meet you. Watching you every Sunday made me believe that with the help of God, *I could . . . I could . . . I could!* Thanks a lot for coming to visit us." He turned away and was lost in the crowd before I could get his name.

You know, some people are chronic complainers. They complain because they have lost something and don't have it anymore. Others complain because they don't have it now and never have had it! Others complain because they're sure they never will have it! Still others complain about "near misses." My daughter Carol, who is eleven years old, got into an elevator with her nine-year-old sister the other day. She got angry at her younger sister and said, "You almost got my foot caught in the door!" I said, "Carol, for goodness sakes, don't complain about the 'almost' troubles that didn't happen!" Surely, God saves people at such times as these! Instead of complaining about accidents that almost happened, thank God that they did not! Stop complaining and then start committing yourself to doing what you would really like to do!

"The only difference between a champ and a chump is 'U'."

III.

The last slogan is, "Yes, Lord, I will." What is that positive thought that has entered your mind? To turn this Beatitude into a life-changing sentence, say, "Yes, Lord, I will do it. Whatever the cost, I will."

How are you living with God right now? Are you following Him? Are you walking with Him? Are you living His life? How real is Jesus Christ to you? Is He your personal friend? Is He your personal Savior? Have you let Him come into your heart? Have you given your life to Him? "Yes, Lord, I should . . . Yes, Lord, I can . . . Yes, Lord, I will." It will cost you something, of course, but if you want to save your life, you will lose it.

Benno Fisher is a good friend of mine. He was an associate architect in the Garden Grove Com-

munity Church. One distinguishing feature about
Benno is a great big tattoo at the top of his left
hand. It says, "K-L." "K" stands for "concentration." "L" stands for "Larga"—Concentration camp. He was one of 4,000 Jews thrown into
a concentration camp during W.W. II. He said
that after a few months, people began dying
around him. Their diet consisted of one bowl of
soup and a 1-inch cube of bread per day.

Benno relates, "A man next to me, who was
close to death, begged me to trade my full cup of
soup for his little cube of bread. I was so hungry.
The soup is what filled the stomach and satisfied
our hunger; the bread did nothing. But I kept
thinking, 'Yes, I should. He is dying; I am not.'
So I traded my soup for his piece of bread."
Benno related further, "This seemed to go on,
day after day. There was always somebody dying.
They always asked me to trade my bowl of soup
for their little piece of bread. I felt so sorry for
them . . . so I traded.

"The day finally came. We heard the distant
rumble of guns and before we knew it, the Amer-
icans were coming! We were free! The war was
over for us! We counted heads, 387 still alive out
of the original 4,000 prisoners! I wondered why
God had let me live. And a doctor answered my
question. 'Why, Mr. Fisher,' he said, 'you lived
because you kept trading your soup for bread!
The bread had enough nutrition in it to keep you
alive! The soup had nothing in it. You did not

enjoy the bread like you would have enjoyed the soup, but it kept you alive!'"

You want a really, truly satisfying life? Then believe in this Beatitude:

"Blessed are they who hunger and thirst for righteousness, for they shall be filled."

> *Blessed is the man who satisfies the deepest hunger in his heart when he utters three life-changing sentences:*
>
> "YES, LORD—I SHOULD."
> "YES, LORD—I CAN."
> "YES, LORD—I WILL."

CHAPTER FIVE

Nothing will make you happier than reaching out to someone who is hurting!

"Blessed are the merciful, for they shall obtain mercy."

(Matt. 5:7)

5

How to Get People to Treat You Beautifully

Jesus gives the key on how to get people to treat you beautifully. The secret is in the Beatitude: "Blessed are the merciful, for they shall receive mercy." (Matt. 5:7)

Here is a fundamental rule of life: *If you want people to treat you nicely, treat them nicely.* Hit a man, and he will hit you back. For every action, there is a reaction. For every positive action, there is a positive reaction. For every negative action, there is a negative reaction. This Beatitude then holds three things—first, a promise; second, a prescription for happy living; and third, a power principle that has universal application. If you really want to discover the key to happiness, look at this Beatitude, and then live it.

I.

First, accept *the promise* of the Beatitude. This is God's promise, that if you treat people mercifully He, God, will be merciful to you. Later, in the Sermon on the Mount, Jesus teaches: *"If you forgive men their trespasses, God will forgive you yours. But if you do not forgive men for the hurts they have caused you, God will not forgive you for the hurt you have caused Him.* If at any point in your life you feel you need the forgiveness of God for something, you will not receive God's forgiveness so long as you harbor resentment against some other person. If you do not forgive men their trespasses, neither will your Father forgive you yours. With what measure you give, it will be given to you.

If you are critical, you can expect people to criticize you. If you gossip about people, you can be sure these same people that you gossiped to are going to gossip about you. "Do not throw your pearls before swine, lest they trample them under foot and turn to attack you." (Matt. 7:6) The promise is, if you want to be treated mercifully, you must be merciful. If you want forgiveness, give it.

Years ago I told a story. Recently a national magazine told the same story but in a modern, updated version which, according to the author, really happened.

According to the modern version, three teenagers boarded a bus in New Jersey. Seated on the bus was a quiet, poorly dressed man who sat alone, unspeaking. When the bus made its first rest stop, everybody got off except this one man, who sat there coldly and alone. When the kids came back on the bus, one of them said something nice to him and he smiled shyly.

At the next bus stop, as everybody got off, the last teenager turned and said to the man, "Come on off. At least stretch your legs."

So he got off and the teenagers invited him to sit with them. One of the young people said, "We are going to Florida for a weekend in the sun. It is nice in Florida, they say." He said, "Yes, it is." Another one said, "Have you been there?" "Oh, yes," he said, "I used to live there." One said, "Well, do you still have a family and a home there?" He hesitated. "I—I don't know," he said, finally. "What do you mean, you don't know?" the teenager persisted. And then caught up by their warmth and their sincerity he shared this story with them.

"Four years ago I was sentenced to Federal prison. I had a beautiful wife and wonderful children. I said to her, 'Honey, don't write to me and I won't write to you. The kids should not know that their Dad is in prison. You go right ahead and find another man, somebody who will be a good father to those boys.'

"She kept her bargain and so did I. Last week, when I knew for sure I was getting out, I wrote a letter to the old address; it's just outside of Jacksonville. I said to her, 'If you are still living there and get this letter, and if there is a chance of you taking me back, here is how you can let me know. I will be on the bus as it comes through town; I want you to take a yellow handkerchief and hang it in the old oak tree right outside of town.'"

One teenager said, "Wow!" and the others said, "Wowee!" When they got back on the bus and they were about ten miles from Jacksonville, all the teenagers moved to his side of the bus and pressed their faces against the windows. Just as they came to the outskirts of Jacksonville there was the big oak tree and the teenagers let out a yell and a scream and they jumped out of their seats. They hugged each other and danced in the center of the aisle. All they said was, "Wowee, wowee, look at it!" There was no yellow handkerchief on the tree, but there was a yellow bedsheet, a yellow dress, a little boy's yellow pants, and yellow pillow cases. *The whole tree was covered with yellow!*

"Blessed are the merciful, for they shall obtain mercy."

That is the way God treats you and me when we treat people right. It is a promise from God that He will forget the past and forget the record we have rolled up. It is a promise that He will throw away the black pages out of our book and give us such a big welcome that you will be reminded of the Prodigal Son's father who said, "My son that was lost is found and is home again." This is the promise of this Beatitude.

II.

The *prescription* for joyful living is very simple —if you want to have joy, treat people right. It is impossible to have thoughts of resentment and jealousy and anger and hate and ill-will, and expect to be happy. You cannot sow these negative emotional seeds and expect to raise a harvest of smiles and whistling laughter. Nobody can be happy and angry at the same time. It is so incredibly simple.

I want to introduce you to one of the persons that may well be the most beautiful person alive in the world today, a person who lives in Calcutta, India. My introduction to her is in a new book, entitled, "Something Beautiful for God."

The story is about Mother Teresa of Calcutta. She is about 60 years old, and she is an amazing person. She was a child of a peasant family in Yugoslavia. She was taken regularly to church, where she met Jesus Christ. As a teenager she felt a calling to go into full-time church work, and she became a Catholic sister. A missionary was telling her congregation in Yugoslavia about the great need to bring Christ to the people in India. So she volunteered and was accepted for a teaching post in Calcutta. At the convent she had enjoyed very lovely quarters. She had beautiful accommodations that were surrounded by lovely gardens. She did her teaching in a very lovely and attractive classroom.

One day she had to make a trip to the dirtiest part of the town. When she walked the streets alone, through the back parts of Calcutta, she saw something she had never seen before. She saw human beings dying and nobody paid attention to them. When she inquired, she found that this was very common. Nobody had time for the dying; nobody had a place for the dying. It haunted her. She felt that Jesus Christ was saying to her, "I am going to call you to serve the poorest of the poor. I am calling you to minister —not to the living, but to the dying."

This was such a strong call that she asked the Church to release her from her vows. It took two years; finally she succeeded and she was released. No longer a nun, she was sent out of the convent and into the streets of Calcutta. With only a few rupees, or pennies, in her pocket, she shuffled down the streets with no promise of a meal and no promise of clothing from the Church. She was on her own, and she prayed, "Jesus, lead me to somebody who is dying all alone."

Two blocks away she saw an old lady lying in the gutter on the main street. The body was half-eaten by the rats that were running in the gutter. She picked up the body and literally dragged it to the nearest hospital. She was refused admittance. "But," she exclaimed, "this woman is dying." She was told, "People die in the streets of Calcutta all the time. We cannot take her." Sister Teresa refused to leave until they had taken the dying woman. She said, "If there is a God in heaven, and a Christ we love, nobody should die alone."

She went to the city government and she asked for an empty room. "A place where I can build a home for the dying," she remarked. The civil authorities answered, "Well, we have this empty Hindu temple of Kali, if that would suit you." She said, "Beautiful. It would be beautiful for God. That is all I want to do in my life, something beautiful for God."

Two other sisters heard about her project, and they helped to drag the dying from the streets into this Hindu temple. Without medicine, without money, without an organization, without any backing, they did what they could, and nobody died in their place without at least a touch on the cheek. "We love you." Kindly words, these! "Go in peace with God." They did not die alone.

Today, Sister Teresa—or Mother Teresa, as she is known—is probably the closest thing to an authentic saint living on planet earth . . . beyond a doubt! She has created her own Sisterhood, called the Missionaries of Charity. It is a pontificate, which means it is now recognized directly below that of the Pope who, when he came to Calcutta to see what this strange ex-nun was doing, was so impressed that he gave her as a gift his own private, expensive white limousine. She took one look at this big, expensive car and she said, "Oh, thank you."

The first thing she did was to announce a raffle. The money went for her house for the dying. Today, she has over 10,000 dying lepers in her colony. Her colonies have spread into 28 cities, to Ceylon, to the Indian people who live in London, in Rome, in Venezuela and in Australia. She and all of those who are members of this new order called "Missionaries of Charity," have taken the vow of total poverty. The only thing they may own is the cheapest cotton garments and a pair of sandals. Total surrender!

My copy of this book has these little stickers on it. Here is the rough face of a Yugoslavian peasant woman turned sister, and it says on these little stickers, "I am Third."

I am third . . .

Christ first.

Others are second.

I'm third.

Malcolm Muggeridge, interviewing her on the British Broadcasting Company and later visiting her in Calcutta, said, "The thing I noticed about you and the hundreds of sisters who now form your team is you all look so happy. Is it a put-on?" She said, "Oh no, not at all. Nothing makes you happier than when you really reach out in mercy to someone who is hurt badly."

III.

A power principle for daily life.

If you want positive things to happen, you must be positive. If you want to be friendly with people and if you want people to be friendly toward you, be friendly to them. It is a universal law. When people come to me and say, "People don't treat me right," investigation almost always shows that they don't treat people right either. It is a law of life.

"Cast your bread upon the waters, for you will find it after many days." (Eccl. 11:1)

"The measure you give will be the measure you get." (Matt. 7:2)

There is this *law of proportionate return.* Your behavior, the words you speak, the gestures you offer, the love you give or don't give, everything —this business of living, is sowing seeds. You throw out a seed when you speak a positive word, when you do something positive. If you are surrounded by undesirable people, change them into good people.

How do you change them into good people?
Bring the best out of them! How do you bring
the best out of them? Call attention to the best
that is within them! *Until they begin to believe
they are beautiful people, they will not treat you
beautifully.*

"Blessed are the merciful, for they shall obtain
mercy." Service is its own reward. A prescription
for joyful living is, "Be good, be kind, be unselfish. Do unto others as you would have them do
unto you."

A promise from God,

   A prescription for joyful living, and . . .

"Blessed are the merciful, for they shall obtain
mercy."

Blessed are the generous; life will be generous
to them. Show me a business that is really suc-
ceeding, and I will show you a business that specializes in really being interested in the customer.
Show me a salesman that is breaking new rec-
ords, and I will show you a man who honestly is
interested in helping to solve people's problems.
People see the sincerity of it and people really
feel he wants to help them. This is a power principle for successful living. Nothing can change it.

If you want to change your world, change
yourself. How do you change yourself? How do
you become this kind of a positive thinking person? I know only one way . . . education does
not do it . . . legislation does not do it. You can

pass all kinds of laws in the state and in the country, but that does not change a human heart. Education does not change the heart. Legislation does not change the heart.

However, there is a living God—and a living Christ who does. Christ can get under a person's skin until that person is born again, and changes. It can happen to you. It happens when you meet Jesus Christ and ask Him to take over your life. It is what Mother Teresa did when she was 14 years old. "Christ, live in me," was her prayer. "Live your life out through me, Jesus Christ."

She did it!

It works!

YOU try it!

CHAPTER SIX

CHRIST IS ALIVE!
Find Him and you will have the greatest experience of your life!

"Blessed are the pure in heart, for they shall see God."

(Matt. 5:8)

6

How to Have a Life-Changing Experience With God

"BLESSED ARE THE PURE IN HEART, *for they shall see God.*"

I could see God tonight

If my heart were right;

If all the rubbish in my soul

Were cleared away; by being whole,

My breast would thrill in glad surprise

To all the wonders in my eyes;

If my heart were right

I could see God tonight.

And in the radiance of His face,

I'd flame with light and fill this place

With beauty, and the world would know

The face of God down here below

Tonight, if my dull heart were right.

    If you have trouble believing in God, you have an emotional problem. Let me prove it to you. Doctor Marais, a leading naturalist, studied the weaverbird from South Africa for years. The weaverbird makes its nest out of reeds, lines it with soft grass and then does what no other bird does, it makes an entrance into the nest from the bottom. Naturalists, of course, have long questioned this innate instinct. Doctor Marais placed two weaverbird eggs under canaries, outside Africa, and waited for them to hatch. They hatched out, and then continued reproduction for five generations. None of these five generations of weaverbirds ever lived in a weaverbird's nest or with another weaverbird. Doctor Marais then took the fifth generation of weaverbirds and returned them to their natural habitat in South Africa. Immediately they searched for reeds and wove a nest; they lined it with soft grass and built an entrance from the bottom.

What does it prove? It is scientific proof of natural instinct. A scientist once said that when God wants to prove something to a creature, He puts it in his instinct and nothing can ever eradicate it. Isn't this the only explanation why Svetlana Stalin, born, bred, raised and indoctrinated in the home of a classical atheist, Joseph Stalin, still found herself in later years incurably religious? I tell you that the Soviet Union may try to keep everybody in atheism for 200 years, but the people will still hunger for religion. God is real and He created us with this religious inclination. You ask, "If this is the case, why don't I believe in God more strongly than I do?" The answer is: Unbelief is an emotional hang-up.

As an example, I want to share the following letter:

"Dear Dr. Schuller: In New York, the time is 1:10 p.m. I have just attended your church by way of television. I must write you now and tell you about my conversion which took place this past Thursday. When you spoke of the seed of grass that had been tossed from its vase and wedged uncomfortably in a crack in the sidewalk, under cement, under the boots of men—well, that was my life, and my early childhood beginning. My parents were well-bred. Money and fame was their god, and they got both. There was always a Bible in my house. I became mentally ill. My parents died and I came to New York. I went through Dr. Peale's clinic, but since I was never able to trust the love of my parents, I was thus never able to trust the love of a supposed God.

"Finally I became aware that Christians are happy; I was not. I knew that somewhere my personality was disconnected. One day I tried to talk to God. I thought my faith was off, so I offered up to Him all that I had: material, talents, skills. I think it was after your sermon where you said, 'I am third—put Christ first, others second, I am third,' that I changed. I said, 'God, I am third, help me.' I did not want to be a sad-sack Christian.

"That following Thursday, Maundy Thursday, I went to a little church. They offered communion and I accepted it. As I took the communion, I asked God to make me a mentally healthy Christian. At that moment it happened. I felt cleansed of all the evil I had carried within me for so long. As I was praying, I saw your smile in my mind, as if God was using the memory of your face to say to me, 'Mary, you have it.' I cannot tell you how happy and relieved I feel."

Then follows her very perceptive P.S.:

"It is a tremendous achievement for the emotionally disturbed person to trust God. I am so glad Christ finally found me.''

Do you want to have a life-changing experience with God? I will give you four points; they are simple and they work. I guarantee it. Four points, they will work for you if you will work with them.

The first point is—WISE UP.

The second point is—CLEAN UP.

The third point is—GIVE UP.

The fourth point is—TAKE UP.

I.

Wise up to one thing: God created man with an instinct to believe. If you do not believe, you have an emotional problem.

Occasionally I meet people who tell me they cannot believe in God because of intellectual blocks. I always ask them these questions:

(1) Is it possible that somewhere in your subconscious there lurks hostility toward your father or your mother?

(2) Is it possible that you have within your subconscious some negative feeling toward your family, your friends, your business associates, or competitors?

(3) Have you ever been hurt by someone who never came back to apologize to you?

(4) Do you have a secret that you have not

shared with any other living human being, about
something you have done, or are doing, or are
thinking about doing, which is either illegal or
immoral?

(5) Have you suffered grief and heartache, and
did your prayers seem unanswered?

(6) Do you feel inferior to others, and do you
have trouble loving yourself?

If you answer *yes* to any one of the questions,
the chances are that you have an emotional problem. You are not free of negative emotion. A
conscious or subconscious negative emotion will
damage, retard, or destroy God-awareness. If
there is within your personality some resentment,
some hostility, some guilt, some fear or some
worry, find it, get rid of it, and you will be surprised to find how much your faith will improve.
How natural it will seem to you to be religious;
as natural and normal as breathing. Negative
emotions block faith, just as the overweight man
won't step on the bathroom scale, or the man
with overdue bills won't look in his mailbox.
Negative emotions block you.

Think of this: If a family problem—maybe a
cross word with your wife or your child—blinds
you from noticing the beautiful new rose which is
blooming outside your front door, isn't it then
easy to realize how a negative emotion lurking
deep within your subconscious can block you
from seeing God who is invisible? If your mind is
so preoccupied with a problem that you are trying to solve, that you do not even notice your

small child standing at your chair talking to you, can't you imagine how your mind's eye can be blocked by a buried negative emotion to an awareness of God's presence?

Now you know why Jesus was such a *powerful believer!* He knew God. Jesus Christ had no emotional blockages! He had no selfish ambitions, no greed, no jealousies, no hatred, no self-pity, no poor selfish griefs. Emotionally He was constantly positive. Wise up! If you are a non-believer, you are not smart . . . you have an emotional problem!

II.

Now—clean up! Get an emotional flushing! Flush the negative emotions out. You will not be able to feel God if you are harboring negative thoughts or negative feelings toward another human being. Remember, Jesus said that if you come to church and suddenly remember you have bad feelings toward a neighbor, get right up, walk out of church and go to that neighbor's house to apologize. Then come back to church and you will be able to make contact with God.

As Leonardo da Vinci was painting the Lord's Supper, one of his aides clumsily spilled some paint at a critical moment . . . da Vinci took a brush in anger and threw it on the floor, and spoke horrible words to the young boy who, distraught, ran out of the studio. Alone and deserted, the artist picked up his brush again and reached to paint the face of Jesus. His hand froze. The creativity was gone. Negative emotion blocks creativity. He finally dropped his brush, went out and wandered around the alleys until he found the sobbing young boy. He put his arm around him and apologized.

"As Christ forgives me, son," he said to the boy, "I forgive you. Come back. We all make mistakes. My mistake of anger was worse than your mistake of spilling the paint." The boy returned with da Vinci. Now, the artist sat down, picked up his brush, and creativity returned as he painted the face of Jesus. That face has been an inspiration to millions ever since.

If there is a negative emotion within you, it is blocking you in your relationship with God. Clean up! "Blessed are the pure in heart, for they shall see God."

TRY THESE EXERCISES

1. Think of some hidden hurt in your past and pray a forgiving prayer for this person. C. S. Lewis said it: "We all agree that forgiveness is a beautiful idea until we have to practice it!"

2. Think of someone of whom you are jealous —pray for his continued prosperity.

3. Think of someone you've hurt, cheated, insulted, slighted, snubbed or criticized. Call him. Invite him to fellowship. Confess to him your un-Christian attitude. Ask for forgiveness.

4. Think of some neglected cause, project, or person. Surprise yourself with a streak of generosity! Really give a lot—of yourself and of your substance.

5. Pray a totally honest prayer to Christ. You doubt God? Tell *Him* so! He'll still love you even if you don't believe in Him! (God specializes in loving sinners!)

Perhaps you read the amazing story of the young Air Force man who is alive today because of the complete change of blood in his body. He had hepatitis; his liver was nearly useless. Doctors drained every cell of blood from this man's body and substituted a saline solution. They lowered his body temperature to 85 degrees. For eight or ten minutes he was, for all practical purposes, physically dead. The doctors then flushed the saline solution out and filled his veins and arteries with new, healthy blood. A medical miracle had occurred—a human life had been saved. Amazing!

Jesus said that if you want to see God, you have to be born again. The old blood is drawn out, a spiritual saline solution is put in, and then the new spirit of Jesus Christ, like new blood, flows through the entire nervous and emotional system; and you become a new person! *"If any man is in Christ, he is a new creature."* Through the Holy Spirit you receive new blood in every cell. If doctors in Texas could give new life to an Air Force man, just imagine what God could do inside your mind!

III.

Wise up! . . . Clean up! . . . Then, Give up!

Blessed are the pure in heart . . . give up anything which you think might be blocking you from a clear relationship with God. I witness to you that the times I felt closest to God were the times when I gave up something I desired very much. It proves the words of our Lord who said, "If any man would come after me, let him deny himself and take up his cross and follow me." (Matt. 16:24)

Recently I went on a fast. For six days I had no solid foods, all with my doctor's enthusiastic approval. I felt close to Jesus Christ. I remember the first time I began tithing, giving God ten per cent of my earnings. Boy, was it tough! I had to give up something; but I did feel close to God! Years ago I smoked. Being one hundred per cent a Hollander, it was perfectly all right. In my childhood church all good Dutch preachers smoked cigars or pipes. I became convinced that, for me, it was not right, and I gave it up. I felt great. You see, it was the principle of doing something with God's help and making it a success. It was an adventure of walking by faith, and God proved himself to me. Wow!

Give up something that you like very much. It may be money . . . it may be smoking . . . it may be eating . . . it may be sex. I do not know what it may be; it is a decision between you and God. Make it a spiritual adventure and you will have an experience with Him. Many people have a low faith level simply because they are scared to stick their necks out with God! Try it!

There he hung on a cross, dying. A scorner, looking up, said of Jesus, "Hah, look at him. He saved others, himself he cannot save." Of course, *there is a universal principle that asserts that there is no salvation without sacrifice.* I do not think you will ever have a real experience with God until you pick out something very dear to you, something you thought you could never do without, and give it up. Give it up . . . with the help of God.

IV.

Wise up, Clean up, Give up, and lastly, *TAKE UP*—the great cause of Christ. What is a pure-hearted person? Somebody who is constantly sin-less? Of course not. That is not what Jesus meant. What is a perfect field? A perfect field is not a field of ground plowed clean, where not a single weed grows. That is not a pure field. A perfect field is a field where not only are there no weeds, but there are also crops planted and grow-ing—corn, cotton, asparagus, wheat. This is a perfect field. Just to give up something, without then taking up something else only turns you into a negative person. You need the negative and the positive poles before you have power. So take up a cause.

There is only one consuming cause that I can offer you. That is the cause of Christ in our world today. God is alive and Christ is alive, and there are millions who are finding Him. If you have not found Him, you have the greatest experience of your life still coming! I offer to you Jesus Christ as your cause.

Take up a "cause" and it's easy to give up "things". *You can live without something, if you have something to live for.*

A young married couple living in a cheap little apartment are happy. Why? They have a cause—their new married love.

An artist lives in a musty attic, ill-fed, ill-clothed. He is happy because he has a cause to live for . . . his creative artistry! He does not need many material things.

A research scientist who comes to his classroom in baggy pants, with an unshaven face and no tie, isn't interested in expensive suits—he is lost in a cause, that of research and study. *You can get by without a lot of things if you have something great to live for.* Thus Jesus said, "Seek ye the kingdom of God; and all these things shall be added unto you." (Luke 12:31)

Do you want to have a real experience with God? Wise up, Clean up, Give up and Take up the cross of Jesus Christ. God is offering to you a cause, Christ's cause. Jesus needs you.

Christ has no hands but our hands to do His work today.

He has no feet but our feet to lead men on the way.

He has no tongues but our tongues to tell men how He died.

He has no help but your help to draw men to His side.

It is that simple. Have you given your heart to Him? Maybe you are a Christian and have accepted Christ, but God is not real enough to you. Maybe there is something in your heart that needs cleansing. Maybe you have to give up something, or take up something.

I remember so vividly how real God became to me when I started tithing. I get many letters, reiterating the same feelings. These people say, in effect, "I started tithing, giving ten per cent of my income to the church. It is amazing how close God is to me in this! The greatest thing about tithing is that it made my faith come alive!" Remember, James said that faith without works is dead.

I told you earlier about Mother Teresa. In my opinion she has to be one of the most beautiful women alive in the world today. Mother Teresa left the shelter and the security of the nunnery with only five rupees in her pocket. She went out into the poorest of the poor section in the vast city of Calcutta. She found a woman half-eaten by rats, still alive, and dragged her to a hospital. That is how she began her life work. Today she is dedicated to helping the poorest of the poor. Those who have met her say she has a radiant God-filled face. No wonder . . . listen to her.

She writes: "Joy. Joy is prayer. Joy is strength. Joy is love. God loves a cheerful giver.

She gives most who gives joy. The best way to show my gratitude to God is to accept everything, even my problems, with joy. A joyful heart is a normal result of a heart that is burning with love. Never let anything so fill you with sorrow as to make you forget for one moment the joy of Christ risen."

She goes on: "We all long for heaven where God is, but we have it in our power to be in heaven with God right now, at this very moment. But to be at home with God now means loving the unlovely as He does, helping the helpless as He does, giving to those who need as He gives, serving the lonely as He serves, rescuing the perishing as He rescues. This is my Christ. This is the way I live."

God is so real. He will be real to you, too, if you take Christ into your heart. Adopt Mother Teresa's goal to "Do something beautiful for God." Look around you now to help someone who is hurting. Do it for Christ!

I could see God tonight

If my heart were right;

If all the rubbish in my soul

Were cleared away; by being whole

My breast could thrill in glad surprise

To all the wonders in my eyes;

If my heart were right
I could see God tonight.

And in the radiance of His face,
I'd flame with light and fill this place
With beauty, and the world would know
The face of God down here below
Tonight, if my dull heart were right.

CHAPTER SEVEN

Jesus is with you always

"Blessed are they which are persecuted for righteousness' sake, for theirs is the kingdom of heaven."

(Matt. 5:10)

7

How to Turn Your Worst Time into Your Best Time

As I was preparing this chapter, I decided that I had no business talking about it, for I've never been persecuted! I therefore decided to devote this entire chapter to the telling of the story of one of the most persecuted Christians I have known in the 20th century. That is Corrie ten Boom. Her story was written in the book, "The Hiding Place," and it became a major movie.

Her story reads like the spine-tingling thriller that it is. Then this thought entered my mind: Why should I tell you the story of Corrie ten Boom? Why not let her tell the story herself?

I made some long distance calls to the Netherlands. Finally, I made a contact and reached her. She made a personal appearance in our church and her remarks are included in these pages.

Corrie ten Boom led the underground railroad in the Netherlands which helped untold numbers of Jews, who were hounded and hunted by the Gestapo, to find escape in her house where they were hidden in a remote, specially constructed room. So Corrie, her sister and her father hid numbers of Jews who are alive today, who would have been killed in concentration camps.

This, Corrie, her sister and her father did, until the Gestapo caught up with them. They were sentenced to prison and hence the months of persecution.

Now listen to what Corrie had to say to our national television congregation:

"Once I met a parachutist and I asked him, 'When you jumped for the first time, from an airplane to the earth, what did you think?' He said, 'I thought only one thing and that was: It works, it works.' I am going to tell you that it works when you go with Jesus. Some people think that it does not work, and I hope that we will persuade them that they can never trust the Lord too much. The Lord said, 'In the world you shall have tribulation; but be of good cheer, I have overcome the world.' (John 16:33)

"Years ago my grandfather started a prayer meeting for the Jews. Every week he came together with his friends in an old watchmaker's shop. There they prayed for the peace of Jerusalem and the salvation of the Jews. That practice was so unusual that I remember the year when they started, 1844. Today, it is not unusual when Christians pray for the Jews. A hundred years later, in the very same house where my grandfather prayed for the Jews, his son, my father, and four of my grandfather's grandchildren and a great grandson were all arrested because they saved Jewish people in Holland during World War II. Four of them had to die in prisons. I came out alive. It seemed strange not to understand the answer, the divine answer, from a prayer for Jews. I cannot understand it; but that does not matter. We have to be ready for tribulation.

"I can tell you that I never had experienced such a realization of Jesus being with me as during the time when I was in the concentration camp. Ravensbruck, located north of Berlin in Germany, is far away from my home in Holland. The barracks where we lived, my sister Betsy and I, was in the shadow of a crematorium. Every day about 600 bodies were burned there. When I saw smoke go up I asked myself, 'When will it be my time to be killed?'''I did not know beforehand that I should be set free by a miracle of God, and a blunder of man one week before they killed all the women of my age.

"I have looked death in the eyes, not once but often. When you see death in people's eyes, you wake up to reality. What a joy it was that Jesus was with me; that I knew He had died on the cross for the sins of the whole world and also for my sins. I was not afraid. I knew that when they killed me, I would go to the house of the Father with many mansions. I would go into the world of the living. What a joy! I knew the best was yet to be. How can we know how strong and rich we are in Jesus Christ and in His presence? By looking at the cross.

> *At the cross, at the cross*
>
> *Where I first saw the light,*
>
> *And the burden of my sins rolled away.*
>
> *It was there, by faith, I received my sight.*

"Sometimes in that terrible concentration camp we had to stand naked; they stripped us of all our clothes. Seven times I went through that ordeal. The first time was the worst; I could hardly bear it. I never have felt so miserable, so cold, so humble. I said to Betsy, 'I cannot bear this.' Then, suddenly, it was as if I saw Jesus at the cross. The Bible tells us they took His garments. He hung there naked. By my own suffering I could understand the fraction of the suffering of Jesus, and it made me so thankful I could feel as He had felt. Love so amazing, so divine, demands my life, my soul, my all. We must not forget we follow a scarred captain. Should we not have scars?

> *Under His faultless orders, we follow through the street. Lest we forget, Lord, when we meet, Show us your hands and feet.*

"Jesus was with us, with Betsy and me, at the camp. In the morning we had to stand roll call very early. The chief of our barracks was so cruel that she sent us out a whole hour too early. Betsy and I did not go to the square where we had to stand for hours during roll call; we walked around the tent. Everything was black. The ground was made black with coal. The barracks were painted black. The only light we had was from the stars and the moon. Jesus was with us and He talked with us, and He walked with us. Betsy said something, then I said something, then He said something. How? I don't know; but we both understood what Jesus said. There was a little bit of heaven in the midst of hell.

"Once Betsy awoke me in the middle of the night. 'Corrie, God has spoken to me. When we are set free, we must do only one thing. We must bring the Gospel over the whole world. We can tell so much from experience, and that is why people will listen. We can tell them that here we have had real experience that Jesus' light is stronger than the deepest darkness. When we meet people who are in darkness, we can tell them that when they go with Jesus they cannot go too deep. Always deeper are His everlasting arms.' One week later Betsy died. Two weeks later, I was set free.

"Do you understand why I became a tramp for the Lord? I worked; I brought the Gospel into many countries, more than 60. One of the greatest joys was when God sent me to Communist countries. What a joy to strengthen those people! They needed encouragement; they have such a difficult time. There the people know what it means to be persecuted for believing in Jesus. Do you know, I have never seen such strong and happy Christians as they are there. They never asked me, 'Pray for us, for the Lord will help us escape tribulation.' No, they always said, 'Tell the people, wherever you go, to pray for us that God will give us power and strength to go on.' I was so glad that I could tell them from the word of God that there is so much strength in the Bible.

"There are boundless resources in the word of God. I could tell them that we are citizens of heaven. Our outlook goes beyond this world in the hopeful expectation of the coming of the Lord Jesus. The hairs of our head are numbered! That means that even the unimportant things of our lives are under the guidance and care of the

Lord. I could tell them the suffering of this time is not worthy to be compared with the coming glory, when one day He will reveal Himself in full spendor to men. We will be filled with the most tremendous joy and God Himself will wipe away the tears from our eyes.

"Was I allowed to speak in the churches? No. A foreigner may not speak in the churches, only bring greetings. I did. I took 30 minutes to bring greetings to the people there! Often, as we sang the closing hymn, I asked the pastor, 'May I say goodbye?' He would say, 'Yes.' Then I said 'goodbye' a whole hour! Yes, that was a joy! Oh, what a joy to be used by God to show the people the realization of the joy of Jesus's presence.

"Once I asked a friend of mine to come with us to my hotel room so we could have a talk. She said, 'Oh, no, your hotel room is the most dangerous spot in the whole country. There is a hidden secret microphone.' I said, 'Really? Then don't come.' One morning I was praying and thanking the Lord for letting me work in that particular country. Then I prayed, 'God you are a God of miracles. I am going to ask you for a miracle. Give me an opportunity to speak before the Communists. They need the gospel, Lord. They have an eternity to lose or to gain. I cannot find an opportunity.' At that very moment I saw little holes in the floor, like the holes of a pepper box; and suddenly I understood. That was the secret microphone; and I said, 'Thank you, Lord,'

This was the answer. I could bring a message to the Communists. They would listen. They not only listened, they recorded every word and took the tape to their superiors.

"Oh, what a joy it was! I could tell these people: 'Here in my hands I have a book, almost bursting with good news. A book with the answers for your great problems. You share the same problems with all human beings, the problems of sin and of death. In this book is your answer for all that we have to know about Jesus. Here we can know that Jesus died on the cross for the sins of the whole world and also for you. When He died on the cross He bore the punishment for you and me. He not only died, He rose again and He is living with us all the time. He is with us until the end of the world. He will fill our hearts with the Holy Spirit and we will have joy. He makes us victorious over sins. That is your answer. Not only that, He also gives us eternal life, and that is the answer for the death problem.' Oh, what a joy it was to bring that word to these people. I could tell them that the Lord Jesus said, Come unto me all—all, that means you there behind the secret microphone. Isn't it a joy to have a story to tell to the nation, a story of joy, of love? Yes, I was happy that I could reach these people.

"Christian, are you afraid of tribulation? Don't be afraid. Do you know that Paul once said, in II Thessalonians 1:4, 5: '. . . we ourselves boast of you . . . for your steadfastness and faith in all your persecutions and afflictions which you are enduring! . . . You may be made worthy of the kingdom of God, for which you are suffering . . .' Don't be afraid, for God did not give us a spirit of fear, but a spirit of love, and of power, coupled with a sound mind.

"I remember when I was a little girl I once said to my father, 'Daddy, I am afraid that I will never be strong enough to be a martyr for Jesus.' Daddy replied, 'Corrie, when you plan to take a train trip, when do I give you money for the train? Three weeks in advance?' 'No, Daddy, the day that I leave.' Father then said, 'That is what God does. Today you do not need the power and strength to suffer for Jesus; but the moment He gives you the honor of suffering for Him, He will also give you all the strength.' I was happy with his answer and went back to play with my dolls. In the books I have written, I have told how the Lord gave me all the strength and all the grace when I was persecuted and suffered so terribly.

"You have such a beautiful verse that you sing:

Faith of our fathers, holy faith,
I will be true to Thee, till death.

"Every one of you may sing that. Everyone can be true and strong. You say, 'But you don't know me.' No, I don't know you; but I know Him. He will give you the strength that you need. I speak from experience: Jesus is with you always till the end of the world.

"Not long ago, when it was still possible but already very dangerous to enter China, a missionary was asked, 'Are you not afraid?' She replied, 'I am afraid of one thing, that I shall become a grain of wheat, not willing to die.' That is good. I hope that you will feel this way, too. I know that the Lord has all the power and the strength available for you. Yes, also for you young Christians.

"Look at a glove. A glove cannot do anything; it cannot write; it cannot cook, it cannot move. But when your hand is in the glove, then it can do many things, even play the piano. Oh, you say that it is not the glove, but the hand in the glove. Yes, that is so; just as you and I are merely gloves and the Holy Spirit is the hand. The Bible says, '. . . be filled with the Spirit.' (Eph. 5:18) The Bible does not give suggestions, it gives commandments. One of the sweetest commandments of the Bible says, 'Be filled with the Spirit.' Remember that not only must your hand be in the glove, but every finger must be in the right hole. Thusly, every corner of our lives must be filled with the Holy Spirit, not just the center. The Holy Spirit will give us strength, and power, and all we need to be good soldiers for Jesus Christ. But we must surrender all!

The shelf behind the door,

Tear it down, throw it out,

Don't use it anymore.

For Jesus wants your dwelling,

From the ceiling to the floor.

He even wants that little shelf

You keep behind the door!

"Say, are you thinking that maybe it does not work when Jesus is with you? Do you know why you are thinking this? Because you have never tried working with Jesus. Try it. Give yourself to Jesus. Open your heart to Him. In His words, 'Behold, I stand at the door and knock; if any one hears my voice and opens the door, I will come in . . .' (Rev. 3:20) Did you hear His voice this morning? When you say, 'Yes, Lord, come in,' He will come in. He will not let you down. If you must go through dangerous and difficult times, don't be afraid, for Jesus was victor, Jesus is victor and Jesus will be victor forever. He is willing to make you and me more than conquerors in this time. Yes, he is the light of the world. May the love, mercy and power of Jesus Christ by supplied to you abundantly during these days of titanic spiritual warfare. The Lord wins and He is able to hold you up and call to you to triumph in all situations that you face. Hallelujah, Amen!"

Now that you have read Corrie ten Boom's story, let me ask you this question:

Do you feel you're being persecuted more than she was? If God could turn her tragedy into a triumph, don't you believe He can turn your bad time into a glad time, too?

CHAPTER EIGHT

Man was made to be at home with God

"Blessed are the peacemakers: for they shall be called sons of God."

(Matt. 5:9)

8

How to Get People to Sincerely Admire You

"BLESSED ARE THE PEACEMAKERS: for they shall be called the sons of God." (Matt. 5:9)

I recently read the life story of Roland Hayes. Some of you young people may not realize that his was undoubtedly one of the great voices of the Twentieth Century . . . a tremendous concert soloist. He had all the odds against him. He said once, "My mother is the person who taught me how to think positively, and I owe all of my success to her."

Roland Hayes was one of three children born to a Negro family on a 15-acre cotton farm in Tennessee. When Roland was five years old, his father, while felling a tree, was caught under a branch and killed. The mother tried as best she could to train and raise her three boys on their small estate. One day she called the boys together and said, "Boys, you just have to get an education. I have a plan. We are going to hitch up the wagon, go to Chattanooga, get a job, and see to it that you boys get an education."

The next day they hitched up their one horse to the wagon and Roland's mother rode in it. The three boys walked barefoot the 62 miles to Chattanooga, Tennessee. They sang in a choir there. The church choir director, Mr. Calhoun, played a record of Caruso and of Melba for the family. Roland Hayes was so moved that he said, "I believe that God has called me to sing a message of peace and brotherhood around the world." With that inspiration he went on to get a job, and then he enrolled at Fisk University.

While traveling with the college concert singers in Boston, he had a sudden impulse which, to his dying day, he said was from God . . . to drop out and try to get established in Boston. Constantly recurring in his memory were the words of his mother, "Roland, you can do it if you believe you can and if you give your life to God." He got a job as a hotel porter, earned $7.00 a week, brought his mother to Boston and furnished a little apartment which cost him $7.00 a week. He used orange crates for furniture. He concluded that he would never get any place unless he made a name for himself, and so he decided to give a concert—all on his own—in the biggest and the best place, the main auditorium in Boston, Massachusetts.

As he said years later, "I found out nobody ever did anything for me unless I really stuck my neck out and tried to help myself." He tried to find people to sponsor him, but no one would because he was a nobody. He thought and thought and he prayed. Suddenly the bright idea came. He wrote a letter to all the richest people in Boston, introducing himself as Roland Hayes, one of the great concert artists of the future, who was inviting them to his first public American concert, on such and such a date. Tickets, $1.50. The impossible happened—he sold out single-handedly every seat in the auditorium. It was a great success. He personally made $2,000 cash. Someone from Santa Monica, in the audience invited him to California to give a concert. He gratefully accepted.

A music critic approached him and said, "Mr.

Hayes, when you sang, you stirred me as do all of the great concert artists, but you had something more and I cannot put my finger on it." That night in his hotel room the man's comment haunted Roland. What did he have that others didn't have? Could it be his blood? He remembered his old uncle saying to him as they picked cotton, "Roland, your father and me came from Africa, from a line of chiefs. Don't you ever forget that. You got chief's blood in your veins." Roland Hayes prayed that night in Santa Monica and he had a revelation that he would leave America and go to East Africa to try to find the tribe from which he came, and discover what made him unique. He spent the last of his money from the Boston concert to get to London, England, on his way to South Africa.

In England, his money ran out and he had nothing. A friend of the pastor of the Royal Chapel inquired, "Roland, how would you like to sing for my pastor friend, Sunday?" Roland accepted quickly. He sang in the Royal Chapel. He sang the song, "And He Never Spoke a Mumbling Word." Three days later Roland got a telephone call from a friend, who asked, "Have you heard the news?" "No. What?" "Well, you sang in the Royal Chapel Sunday and do you know who was there?" Roland remained silent. "The King and the Queen of England! And they are requesting a command performance at Buckingham Palace." Roland couldn't believe his ears. Two days later he sang for the King and

Queen, and in the audience were Caruso and Melba, two great singers of the time.

Roland Hayes became an overnight success. The year, 1924—everything looked wonderful, including a concert in three weeks at the Beethoven Concert Hall, in Berlin. This concert would undoubtedly establish him as a concert soloist on the continent of Europe. En route to Germany, Roland stopped in Prague. He was called into the American Consul's office. "Mr. Hayes," the consul said, "I have bad news for you. You are going to have to cancel your concert in Germany. The French have taken over the Rhineland and they are holding it with troops made up of Negroes brought from America and from Africa. The Germans are furious. No black-skinned person will be able to sing in Germany at this time. You will have to cancel your concert." "Thank you, Mr. Ambassador," Roland said, "I will surely pray about this." The days passed and he could not bring himself to cancel the concert.

On the night of the concert, Roland and his black accompanist carefully made their way to the auditorium and slipped in through a back door. Once inside, they peered through the curtains and saw that the place was packed to overflowing. Now Roland realized he was an international controversial case. When the curtain went up, Roland Hayes stood in the curve of the baby-grand piano, his accompanist seated at the piano beside him. He quietly folded his hands, looked upward and spoke a private prayer to God.

"God, make me a horn for the Omnipotent to sound through." As he stood silently praying, suddenly he heard the hissing, then stomping, and then the catcalls and boos. Somebody shouted, "Don't disgrace the Beethoven Concert Hall with plantation songs about black men from America."

Hate seemed to fill that auditorium. His piano accompanist said, "Mr. Hayes, we better get out of here." Objects began to fly onto the stage, narrowly missing the soloist. Roland Hayes later recalled the incident and remarked, "I just stood there with my hands folded and prayed, 'God, what will I do?'" A bright idea entered his mind. To the accompanist he said, without taking his eyes off the audience, "Let's begin with the number, 'This is My Peace,' by Beethoven." The accompanist picked it out, the God-inspired first number, and slowly, softly the fingers began to roll across the piano. The German people began to listen to the music of their favorite, Beethoven. Roland Hayes opened his mouth and he began to sing, "This is my peace." His voice rolled through the auditorium; the audience quieted down. When he finished, there was absolute attention. From there he sang classical numbers and ended with Negro spirituals, the plantation songs. At the close of the concert, some members of the audience jumped up on the stage, hoisted Roland on their shoulders and paraded him around the auditorium. He was the hero of the continent, and he was an inspiration in settling the dispute between France and Germany.

"Blessed are the peacemakers: for they shall be called the sons of God." The word, you know, is peace-maker and not just peace-talker.

The Garden Grove Community Church took on the project of helping to build a $125,000 high school in the province of Que Chang, in Southern Korea. It is a school born of a dream by my classmate in seminary. Chun Yung Chang. I met Chun quite by chance sometime ago and discovered that he was teaching high school in a building which leaked so badly that the students held umbrellas to keep the water off their paperwork on their desks. I said to Chun, "Come to America; let us help you. Give us the privilege of being your partners in building a new, modern school." At our insistence, he accepted the invitation and today the school stands as a living example of my friend Chun.

One thousand students and parents crowded onto their playground for the ceremony. Chun did not talk about peace all the time. He didn't talk against war. He did not say he was against poverty. Why not? He believes in acting, not talking. He positively got at the root cause of poverty and of war and of conflict through education. Not far from Chun Yung Chang's province is North Korea. They talk of peace, but wage war. If the South Koreans stand up in self-defense, the North Koreans will accuse them of waging war and causing bloodshed.

Who are the real peacemakers? I can assure you it is not the Communists of North Korea. It was men like Chun Yung Chang . . . men who are making something, creating something, building something . . . not just talking, and walking, and marching, and protesting. Chun built a school where young men and women could be educated so that they might accumulate money instead of living in poverty; so that they might be leaders in a society with a belief in God, in Jesus, in the family, and in freedom. The greatest peacemakers I know do not talk a lot about peace, because they are busy building things that will help human beings. When you help persons to have a fulfilled life, you are getting at the very root cause of conflict.

How many of you know the story of Romana Banuelos? You have probably heard the name. Romana Banuelos was the 34th Treasurer of the United States, appointed by President Nixon. She came under fire by the Senate Investigating Committee due to an accusation that she was responsible for the hiring of 36 wetbacks. Thirty-six illegal Mexican aliens, it was said, were found working in her factory. She was accused of exploiting wetbacks for cheap labor. Romana went to Washington to refute the accusation. She produced facts to show that of the 36 aliens arrested in her plant of over 300 employees, all but two were card-carrying union members. The two who were not union members had been endorsed by the union since they were applying for union membership at the time. All 36 Mexican aliens had signed application work forms, claiming the United States as a legal place of residence. Mrs. Banuelos was paying her employees wages equivalent to those of the highest paid union employee in Southern California in that particular line of work.

Furthermore, the story of Romana Banuelos became better known. Born in Mexico, married at 16 and the mother of two little boys by the time she was 19; divorced at the age of 20. Determined to support her boys, she went to El Paso and worked for $1.00 a day in a laundry. She could not feed her children on $1.00 a day in 1943 in El Paso. Then she heard there was money in the streets of Los Angeles. She let her grandmother take care of the boys and she left. She arrived at the bus depot with $7.00 in her purse and the address of someone who once knew her mother.

She waved down a taxi, got in, and gave the driver the address. Six dollars and sixty-six cents later, Mrs. Banuelos arrived at her destination, with only 34 cents in her purse. The next day she walked the streets and begged for work. A restaurant owner said, "If you will wash these dishes, I will pay you cash." For ten straight hours she stood on her feet until she had washed all the dishes. She earned $8.00 and thanked God for it. She took that $8.00 and went out to find more work, and she washed more dishes. She got another job and she scrubbed toilets. Finally she got a job in a little taco business which was owned by two unscrupulous men who really exploited her. They knew she could not understand English and they took advantage of her. They said, "How would you like to buy our business?" Innocently, she said, "Yes, I guess so." She borrowed $400 from an aunt. They put a contract in front of her to sign, selling their nearly bankrupt business for $2,500. Now she had a business and had to begin work at 2:00 a.m. making tacos. From two in the morning until ten at night, day after day, seven days a week, month after month, she labored until finally she bought the business outright. She owned a business. Her aunt quit. She was 23 years old.

From that sour beginning, Romana Banuelos has dedicated her life to her children and to her God and to what she believed in. Today her business is a $5 million a year proposition. She employs 300 people, at the highest salary scale, and she says, "There are brown berets that are saying they are for peace and racial peace; but they are only Communists. I am for peace. I teach my people how to work. I create jobs for them and and I give them money and pride, and they buy houses and nice clothes for their children. A husband is at peace with his wife; the parents are at peace with their children, because they have a house, and carpets, and clothes, and a car. I make peace in my own way."

"God bless you; God bless you," is my reply. It is what I also said to Chun Yung Chang. It is what I say to people like Roland Hayes. It is

what I say to people like Leon Sullivan, in
Philadelphia. In my mind he must be one of the
ten greatest Negroes alive in America today. Today there are all kinds of agitators. Leon Sullivan
wanted to make peace among the troubled hearts
in a racially tense climate. He saw what the problem was: poverty. Deeper than that, behind poverty, he saw ignorance. Leon Sullivan decided to
set up "Opportunity Industrial Center." He took
his people who were leaning on lampposts in
Philadelphia and said, "Come, I will teach you
how to lay bricks. I will teach you how to
straighten out a fender. I will teach you how to
use a typewriter. I will teach you how to wear a
shirt. I will teach you how to comb your hair. I
will teach you how to wear clothes. I will teach
you how to go into the white man's business, and
the owner will be so impressed that he will want
to hire you." Because of that kind of philosophy,
Leon Sullivan was on the Board of Directors of
the General Motors Corporation. He was also a
most dynamic preacher and pastor of a Baptist
church on the East Coast. His church was filled
to overflowing every week.

Who are the peacemakers? Those who are doing something, creating something, building
something to help people become fulfilled, complete persons, whole human beings. Who are the
real peacemakers? Probably not the people who
are talking about peace all the time. Maybe people like you Christians, and myself—who, in our
own ways, are trying to bring Jesus Christ into

human hearts. There can be no peace in your marriage, if your heart is at war. You are not going to be at peace with your employer and your job, if you are fighting something inside. You are not going to have peace in your family until you have peace in your mind. There is no one who can do a more beautiful job of putting peace into your heart, and in your soul, than Jesus Christ.

The gospel of Christianity is this: Man was made to be at home with God like a fish is at home in water. But there is sin in all of our lives —it is selfishness, and all kinds of things: it is greed, it is jealousy, it is self-pity, it is lust, it is all of this; it is sin! Sin keeps us away from God. You probably would be afraid to sit down to dinner with Amy Vanderbilt for fear that you might do something impolite. Similarly, knowing you are not perfect, you are afraid and tend to stay away from God.

Jesus came into the world to die on a cross to save you from your sins. He can come by the Holy Spirit into our lives. He transforms a human being, and we no longer fear God. We love Him. We want to embrace Him. As the Old Testament prophet said, "Thou wilt keep him in perfect peace, whose mind is stayed on thee; because he trusteth in thee." (Is. 26:3)

When we accept Jesus Christ, we feel at home with God. We then know what Jesus meant when He said, "Peace I leave with you, my peace I give unto you: not as the world giveth, give I unto you. Let not your heart be troubled, neither let it be afraid.'' (John 14:27)

Find peace of mind, now.

Shalom, may peace be with you.